THE VIRGIN BIRTH

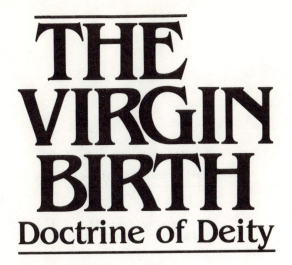

THE VIRGIN BIRTH

Doctrine of Deity

ROBERT G. GROMACKI

BAKER BOOK HOUSE
Grand Rapids, Michigan 49506

First printing, June 1981
Second printing, February 1984

PHOTOLITHOPRINTED BY CUSHING - MALLOY, INC.
ANN ARBOR, MICHIGAN, UNITED STATES OF AMERICA

To

the three "G's"

in my life

GLORIA

GARY

GAIL

CONTENTS

PART V   THE PURPOSES OF THE VIRGIN BIRTH

PART VI   THE DENIALS OF THE VIRGIN BIRTH

PREFACE

When I was approached by Thomas Nelson Inc., Publishers, to do a volume on the virgin birth of Jesus Christ, I immediately thought of the classic evangelical defense of that doctrine by J. Gresham Machen, entitled *The Virgin Birth of Christ*. Ever since its original publication in 1930, it has enjoyed a continuous printing history. Produced in the heat of the liberal-fundamentalist controversy of the first third of this century, it has stood, like Mount Everest, unsurpassed by subsequent evangelical books on the subject and unanswered by liberal scholarship. Who, then, was I to attempt a volume on this critical tenet of the evangelical faith?

Throughout my twenty-three years of formal training and college teaching, I not only was pointed to Machen's book as the final word on the subject, but I also directed my students to it. Yet strangely enough, I had never read it. In fact, I didn't own a copy. Inquiring of my colleagues, I discovered that most of them had not read it and that the minority had only sampled it. When I read through the book, I discovered the reason for this strange paradox. In contemporary jargon, it is a "heavy" book. It is difficult to read because Machen, writing out of his superior intellect and wide range of research, wrote for readers who were also acquainted with the critical liberal approach to the Scriptures, especially the synoptic Gospels. The average layman of today would doubtless be discouraged after reading one or two chapters with little or no understanding and therefore would put the book down. Even trained seminarians would struggle with its contents. This problem of communication should not be blamed upon Machen. His book, ably written, met a definite need in his day. The book *is* a gold mine of Scriptural truth and logic, but it requires a great deal of work to dig it out. I came away from my reading, encouraged to produce a volume that would deal with the virgin birth of Christ on a level understandable to both the interested layman and the formally trained Bible student. Consequently, some areas ably treated by Machen (e.g., the literary integrity of the birth narratives) are only briefly alluded to in this volume. In some places, there is noticeable disagreement (e.g., the genealogies). Most of the material in this book was not developed by Machen (e.g., the relationship of the virgin birth to the hypostatic union of the two natures within Christ). This study will be strongly Biblically orientated. It is undertaken with the conviction that the Bible is the inscripturated Word of God, the only authoritative basis of our faith.

I am convinced that the doctrine of the virgin birth of Jesus Christ with its vital connection to the person of the incarnate Son of God is misunderstood both by its opponents and advocates. Few evangelicals can correctly state the orthodox position on the trinity and the relationship of the divine nature to the human nature within Christ's person. Test yourself with this true or false statement: "Jesus Christ has the same essence and nature as God the Father, but He is not the same Person." Try this one also: "Jesus Christ possessed two natures, human and divine, and two personalities, human and divine." The first was true, but the second was false. Students, from Christian homes and evangelical churches, have consistently missed those when they appeared on my exams. It is my prayer and hope that God will use this book to bring His children into a more mature knowledge of His Son and of His dramatic entrance into the world almost two thousand years ago.

Special thanks are extended to Bill Cannon, religious editor of Thomas Nelson, who invited me to undertake this project. My appreciation and love go to my dear wife, Gloria, who faithfully typed this manuscript from my handwritten text in the midst of her many other duties as housewife, mother, and elementary teacher.

All Scripture quotations are taken from the 1611 Authorized Version, commonly known as the King James Version. References to the Greek text are based upon *The Greek New Testament,* printed by the United Bible Societies.

ROBERT GLENN GROMACKI

THE VIRGIN BIRTH
Doctrine of Deity

INTRODUCTION

"What think ye of Christ? whose son is he?" (Matt. 22:42). That question, asked by Christ of the Pharisees, has been voiced in every generation ever since Jesus walked on this earth. The Jewish religious leaders believed that the promised Messiah would be the Son of David, a human member of the royal family. He would be that, nothing more and nothing less. They rejected the notion that the Christ could also be God. They charged Jesus with blasphemy because he claimed to be the Son of God as well as the son of David. This denial has persisted for nineteen centuries. The questions have been worded differently (and wrongly, in most cases), but the answers have remained the same. How could God become a man? How can one person be both divine and human at the same time? Atheists, skeptics, and liberal Christendom have united in their denunciation of the incarnation of the Second Person of the trinity. To them, it is irrational that the trinity could exist. To them, it is illogical that God could become flesh. Many of these celebrate the birth of Jesus each year at Christmas, but they do not acknowledge His virgin conception and birth. They sing the carols enthusiastically without affirming their content.

> Christ, by highest heaven adored
> Christ, the Everlasting Lord!
> Late in time behold Him come,
> Offspring of the Virgin's womb:
> Veiled in flesh the Godhead see;
> Hail th' Incarnate Deity,
> Pleased as man with men to dwell,
> Jesus, our Emmanuel.
> Hark! the herald angels sing,
> Glory to the newborn King.

These critics simply do not believe literally these words. They do not take them in their normal, ordinary meaning. The denial of Christ's deity and His virgin birth is far more subtle today than many gullible Christians suspect.

The Anglican bishop, John A. T. Robinson, received international notoriety when his controversial book *Honest to God* was released in 1963. In a subsequent publication, *But That I Can't Believe!*, he stated: ". . . I accept as strongly as anyone what the New Testament writers are seeking to affirm by the Virgin Birth or the Resurrection." [1] The average reader might be led to think that Robinson embraces the orthodox position on these two cardinal doctrines, but he would be greatly mistaken. Later, Robinson concluded: "But I believe strongly that a Christian can be *free* to say that the bones of Jesus lie around somewhere in Palestine. For the conviction of Christ's living power—which is what belief in *the Resurrection* means—does not *turn* on any theory of what happened to the body." [2] How can you have a resurrection with the bones still in the ground? To the evangelical, this is an obvious contradiction, but the liberal can maintain a symbolical or spiritual resurrection of Jesus and deny a historical, bodily resurrection. He further claims that this is the essence of the creedal statement: I believe in the resurrection of Jesus Christ from the dead. The same holds true for Robinson's paradoxical approach to the virgin birth. He denies that God literally became man via a biological miracle, but he does believe that God can be seen in Jesus of Nazareth. The issue turns on religious semantics and upon the meanings he superimposes upon doctrinal terms. Thus, "virgin birth" does not mean to the liberal Robinson what it means to the evangelical Machen.

If surveys mean anything, the majority of professing Christians reject the historical literalness of the virgin birth. More than a decade ago, the publishers of *Redbook* employed pollsters to investigate the doctrinal beliefs of students in Protestant seminaries. The August, 1961, issue reported that 56% rejected the concept of the virgin birth. The Survey Research Center of the University of California at Berkeley contrasted various denominations in their poll.[3] Registering affirmation in the virgin birth were Congregationists: 21%; Methodists: 34%; Episcopalians: 39%; Disciples of Christ: 62%; United Presbyterians: 57%; Lutherans: 66%; American Baptists: 69%; Lutherans, Missouri Synod: 92%; and Southern Baptists: 99%. Actually, nineteen percent of the Roman Catholics polled rejected the doctrine of the virgin birth.

The evangelical should not be unduly alarmed at such denials. Paul wrote: "For what if some did not believe? shall their unbelief make the faith of God without effect? God forbid: yea, let God be true, but every man a liar . . ." (Rom. 3:3–4a). The factuality of Christ's virgin birth stands in spite of Pharisaical or contemporary liberal denial. The origin of Jesus' humanity is the central question. If He was born apart from male parentage, then He must be God manifest in the flesh. If He were not virgin born, then He was not God. These answers are not mere academic issues. They are *eternal* life and death matters. The rejection of Christ's deity and His virgin birth caused the Pharisees to die in their sins and to receive everlasting judgment (John 8:24). The same is true of the modern liberal.

On another occasion near Caesarea Philippi, Jesus asked His disciples: "Whom do men say that I the Son of man am?" (Matt. 16:13). The answers varied: John the Baptist resurrected, Elijah, Jeremiah, or some other prophet. In each case, He was identified as a holy man, a spokesman for God, but only a mere man. He was not God speaking! Then Jesus became more direct: "But whom say ye that I am?" (Matt. 16:15). To this, Peter, in behalf of the apostolic group, replied: "Thou art the Christ, the Son of the living God" (Matt. 16:16). Peter identified Jesus Christ as both the son of man and the Son of God. How did he arrive at this conclusion? Jesus explained: "Blessed art thou, Simon Bar-jona: for flesh and blood hath not revealed it unto thee, but my Father which is in heaven" (Matt. 16:17). Peter had been blessed by God in that He had opened the disciple's spiritual understanding to perceive the uniqueness of the person of Jesus Christ. No man in his natural intellect and insight can know the things of God; they appear as irrational foolishness to him (1 Cor. 2:9–14). The deity of Christ is one of those "things of God." So, also, are His incarnation, virgin birth, and the resultant union of two natures in His single person. Such truths are hidden from "the wise and prudent" (Matt. 11:25), the Pharisaical types who think that they need no spiritual instruction. Genuine faith in Christ can only come from a babe-like mental and moral stance.

The blessing or the curse of God rests upon an individual in direct proportion to his acceptance or rejection of Christ's deity. This is why John F. Walvoord, the president of Dallas Theological Seminary, said: "The incarnation of the Lord Jesus Christ is the central fact of Christianity. Upon it the whole superstructure of Christian theology depends." A real incarnation requires a literal virgin birth. They are "two sides of the same coin." You can't have one without the other. For years, fundamentalists have been marked by their acceptance of these major doctrinal concepts, the inspiration of the Scriptures, the deity of Jesus Christ, His virgin birth, His substitutionary atonement, His bodily resurrecton, and His second coming to the earth. They come as a doctrinal package. You either embrace all of them or deny them all. No one can logically believe in some of them while rejecting the others.

"But whom say ye that I am?" (Matt. 16:15). And, "What think ye of Christ? whose son is he?" (Matt. 22:42). You, the reader, must *now* answer these questions. Your answers will affect your eternal destiny.

1 Where Do We Start? (The Trinity)

Does God exist? If He does, what is He like? Answers to these questions provide clues for the theoretical possibility of the virgin birth. If the atheist is correct, then naturally there could be no incarnation. If the world is controlled by many gods (polytheism), then you could have *an* incarnation of *a* god. This, however, is altogether different from *the* incarnation of *the* one and only God of the universe. The hyper-monotheistic concept of Judaism and Protestant liberalism would also rule out a genuine incarnation. Otherwise, you would have a situation in which the incarnate God would be praying to Himself. This is both ridiculous and unscriptural.

Starting Point

The monotheistic, trinitarian concept of God, as embraced by Protestant orthodoxy and the Roman Catholic Church, provides the only logical starting point. Samuel Mikolaski, former professor of theology at the New Orleans Baptist Theological Seminary, rightly stated: "Even more crucial is the problem of how to fit in the Incarnation unless God is triune. Do not Christians confess the twin truths that God sent his Son into the world and that God is revealed incarnate in Jesus Christ?" [1]

It is one thing to say it; it is another to prove it. How can God be both one and three? How can monotheism and trinitarianism be harmonized? How can the infinite God be explained by finite man? Can the thing made define the essence of its maker? Zophar correctly quizzed Job: "Canst thou by searching find out God? canst thou find out the Almighty unto perfection?" (Job 11:7). Man can't understand himself completely, let alone God. The series in the *Readers' Digest* entitled "I Am Joe's Body" has created a spirit of awe within the mind of man. From the tiniest cell to the most complex organ, he is a living marvel. With the Psalmist, he must conclude: "I will praise thee; for I am fearfully and wonderfully made: marvellous are thy works; and that my soul knoweth right well" (Ps. 139:14). Both the anatomist and the psychologist wonder at the complex organism known as "man." If man can't search out himself totally, how can he explain God adequately? If he tries to do it out of his own ingenuity, he will utterly fail. This is the error of liberalism. It attempts to understand the nature of God by reconstructing Him from what it knows of man. This is why atheists charge man with the creation of God in his own image.

The only way for man to have an adequate, working knowledge of the nature of God is for God to reveal Himself to man. Jesus said: ". . . no man knoweth the Son, but the Father; neither knoweth any man the Father, save the Son, and he to whomsoever the Son will reveal him" (Matt. 11:27). Since the Scriptures testify of the Son (John 5:39) and the Son testifies of the Father, these two testimonies must agree. All Scripture is inspired or God-breathed (2 Tim. 3:16); therefore, God has revealed Himself to man through the written Word, the Bible. To have a true but partial understanding of God's essence (1 Cor. 13:12), a person must submit his rational powers to the authoritative voice of the Scriptures. God must be permitted to explain Himself to man. No man should expect to know everything about the nature and activities of God. His finite mind can't fathom or contain the omniscience of God. If there are concepts that he doesn't totally understand, he must not blame God or the Biblical writers. He should not regard them as irrational, but supra-rational. God Himself said: "For my thoughts are not your thoughts, neither are your ways my ways, saith the Lord. For as the heavens are higher than the earth, so are my ways higher than your ways, and my thoughts than your thoughts" (Isa. 55:8–9). In such moments of finiteness, the spiritual man will respond: "O the depth of the riches both of the wisdom and knowledge of God! how unsearchable are his judgments, and his ways past finding out! For who hath known the mind of the Lord? or who hath been his counsellor?" (Rom. 11:33–34).

Scriptural Proof for Trinitarianism

The oneness of God is taught throughout the Scripture. Monotheism was commanded of Israel (Ex. 30:3). Later, Moses declared: "Hear, O Israel: The Lord our God is one Lord: And thou
shalt love the Lord thy God with all thine heart, and with all thy
soul, and with all thy might" (Deut. 6:4–5). Polytheism was expressly forbidden. Only if God were one could a person love and
worship Him with his total being all of the time. If there had
been three gods, then an individual could love one of them with
his entire person to the exclusion of the other two. Or, he could
give each of the three gods one third of his devotion at any one
time. However, he could never give three different gods his total
worship at the same time. The prophets constantly called the back-
slidden Israelites from their idolatrous practices to a worship of
the one Jehovah (Isa. 43:10–11; 44:6; 45:5). Jesus declared the
oneness of God (Mark 10:18; 12:29 cf 12:32). Paul rejected the
reality of false gods and idols and affirmed the oneness of God
also (1 Cor. 8:4–6; 1 Tim. 2:5). James argued: "Thou believest
that there is one God; thou doest well; the devils also believe, and
tremble" (James 2:19). There is no indication that the concept
of monotheism changed or evolved from the Old Testament to the
New Testament. Paul, Peter, and the other Christians claimed to
worship the same one God that Adam, Abraham, David, and the
other Old Testament saints adored. Monotheism is essential to a
proper definition of trinitarianism and to a logical basis for the
incarnation.

Since God is one in His basic essence, how can He also be
three? First, it must be pointed out that "one" and "three" are
not being used in the same sense. The word "one" applies only
to the nature of the divine Being; there is only one God. The word
"three" refers to the three Persons or personal distinctions within
the divine oneness. It is just as wrong to state that God is one Person as to claim that there are three gods.

The Old Testament definitely implied the existence of more than
one Person within the divine oneness. The first clue is to be found
in one of the Hebrew names for God—*Elohim.* Found in the first
verse of the Bible (Gen. 1:1), it is used repeatedly by the Old

Testament writers. The *im* in *Elohim* is a plural suffix added to the singular noun *El*. Some have called this literary phenomenon "the plural of majesty," but isn't God's singular name *El* majestic enough? In the temptation, Satan enticed Eve: ". . . ye shall be as gods [*Elohim*]" (Gen. 3:5). The word "gods" should have been translated "God," a reference to the God of creation. A second hint is found in plural pronouns ascribed to God. God said: "Let *us* make man in *our* image" (Gen. 1:26; italics mine). This usage of the first personal plural pronouns also occurs elsewhere (Gen. 3:22; 11:7; Isa. 6:8). To explain them away as joint references to God and His angels or to an editorial "we" is just too simplistic. In fact, both the oneness of God and the plurality of Persons are taught in these passages. After God said: "Let us make man in our image, after our likeness" (Gen. 1:26), Moses wrote: "So God created man in his own image" (Gen. 1:27). Isaiah "heard the voice of the Lord saying, Whom shall I send, and who will go for us?" (Isa. 6:8). Note the interchange of the singular and the plural in both of these incidents. Since God is one, He can say "I." Because of the plurality of Persons, He can also say "us." A third clue is in the usage of the word "one" (cf. Deut. 6:4). It can be used in two different ways: one person or one people. The latter implies that there is more than one person within the singular group. Such usage is common (Gen. 2:24; Ex. 24:3; 26:11; Judg. 6:16; Ezek. 37:19). These reveal a plurality in unity, not a single undiversified sameness.

The number of Persons within the oneness of the divine being cannot be determined from the above study. There could be two, three, four, etc. It can only be safely stated that there is more than one Person within the Godhead. The concept of three Persons is based upon these interpretations. First, God admonished Aaron through Moses to pronounce this blessing: "The Lord bless thee, and keep thee: The Lord make his face shine upon thee, and be gracious unto thee: The Lord lift up his countenance upon thee, and give thee peace" (Num. 6:24–26). Here is a triple blessing with a triple mention of God's name. Second, Isaiah heard the seraphim cry: "Holy, holy, holy, is the Lord of hosts" (Isa. 6:3). This triple invocation coupled with the plural pronoun usage argue for three Persons.

In the Old Testament, there is an identification of "the angel of the Lord" with "God." After the angel of the Lord discovered Hagar in the wilderness and spoke with her, she reacted in this way: "And she called the name of the Lord that spake unto her, Thou God seest me" (Gen. 16:7–12 cf. 16:13). She equated the two. So did Abraham (Gen. 22:11–15 cf. 22:16). It was the angel of the Lord who appeared to Moses in the burning bush and who named Himself "I am" (Ex. 3:2, 4, 14 cf. John 8:58). He doubtless is "the messenger of the covenant" (Mal. 3:1), a reference to the Messiah who would cleanse the Levites at His coming into the temple. The "angel of the Lord" is recognized as God and yet can be distinguished from God. Since there are no appearances of "the angel of the Lord" in New Testament times, He has been equated with God the Son in a pre-incarnate manifestation. Thus, He could be called God and yet be distinct from God the Father.

Through Isaiah was revealed a distinction of three Persons: "Come ye near unto me, hear ye this; I have not spoken in secret from the beginning; from the time that it was, there am I: and now the Lord God, and his Spirit, hath sent me" (Isa. 48:16 cf. 61:1). In themselves, these verses do not establish beyond a shadow of doubt that these three Persons can all be called divine (Lord God, Spirit, me). This equation, however, was made in the New Testament.

In the divine program of progressive revelation, the Old Testament stressed the monotheistic nature of God whereas the New Testament emphasized the Trinitarian concept, clarifying the prior allusions to the plurality of persons. The trinity could now be seen clearly. At the baptism of Jesus, all three Persons were active. The Spirit of God descended upon Jesus and the voice of the Father declared: "This is my beloved Son, in whom I am well pleased" (Matt. 3:17). Jesus, in His teaching, made this distinction: "But when the Comforter is come, whom I will send unto you from the Father, even the Spirit of truth, which proceedeth from the Father, he shall testify of me" (John 15:26 cf. 14:16, 26). The resurrected Christ charged the apostles to baptize "in the name of the Father, and of the Son, and of the Holy Ghost" (Matt. 28:19). God is one, so the name is singular, but since there are three Persons within the divine being, they are distinguished as Father, Son, and Spirit. The three Persons are later associated by Biblical writers in the administration of Spiritual gifts (1 Cor. 12:4–6; Spirit, Lord, God), in a benediction (2 Cor. 13:14; Lord Jesus Christ, God, Holy Ghost), in the program of human redemption (1 Peter 1:2; God the Father, Spirit, Jesus Christ), and in the preservation of Christian experience (Jude 20–21; Holy Ghost, God, Lord Jesus Christ). These passages show that there is not a set order for the appearance of the names of the three Persons. This reveals the equality of the three Persons. Within the divine oneness, the Father is not superior to the Son or the Spirit, nor is the Son superior to the Spirit. All three Persons are named as God: the Father (Rom. 1:7), the Son (Heb. 1:8), and the Spirit (Acts 5:3–4). Since the Bible denies the existence of three separate gods, the above passages must teach a trinity in unity, a plurality of persons within the divine oneness. This distinction is vital to the nature of the incarnation and to the method of the virgin birth. It was not the entire trinity that became incarnate; it was not the Person of the Father nor the Person of the Spirit; it was the Person of the Son who became flesh.

Doctrinal Statement

The doctrine of the trinity is a Biblical mystery, a truth revealed by God. No man by a detailed study of nature and of his own personality would have concluded that the nature of God was trinitarian. It is beyond his rational powers that such a God could exist. The problem of understanding is further compounded when theologians try to communicate the "definition" or "description" of God to others. What words, out of a human vocabulary, can be chosen? Many words are not static; their meanings tend to change with the passing generations. Still other words can mean different things to different people.

The early church had to face this problem when it attempted to put into creedal statement its belief in the Biblical teaching of the trinity. The Athanasian Creed (fourth century) stated: "We worship one God in Trinity, and Trinity in Unity; neither confounding the Persons, nor dividing the Substance." The church fathers used the words "one," "unity," and "substance" to stress their belief in monotheism. Likewise, they employed the words "trinity" and "persons" to indicate their belief in trinitarianism. They were careful to point out that God could not be divided into three parts and that the three Persons should not be identified with each other. The Nicene Creed (A.D. 325) was more explicit: "We believe in one God—and in one Lord Jesus Christ, the Son of God, begotten of the Father, light of light, very God of very God, begotten, not made, being of one substance with the Father—and in the Holy Ghost." The Nicene-Constantinople Creed (A.D. 381) reaffirmed this position. These creeds stood for centuries as the standard of doctrinal orthodoxy.

When the Protestant Reformation broke over Europe in the sixteenth century, there developed a need for the emerging denominational groups to express their views on the being of God. The Augsburg Confession (A.D. 1530) reflected the attitude of Martin Luther and of the Lutheran Church: "There is one Divine essence which is called and is God, eternal, without body, indivisible, of infinite power, wisdom, goodness, the Creator and Preserver of all things, visible and invisible, and yet there are three Persons of the same essence and power, who also are coeternal, the Father, the Son, and the Holy Ghost." Later, the Thirty-Nine Articles (A.D. 1571) were published by the Church of England as a statement of its faith. Used also by the Protestant Episcopal Church in the United States, one relevant sentence reads: "There is but one living and true God. And in the unity of the Godhead there are three Persons, of one substance, power, and eternity, the Father, the Son, and the Holy Ghost." The Westminster Confession (A.D. 1647) of the Presbyterian Church, also adopted in the Canon of the Synod of Dort by the Reformed Church, stated: "There is but one living and true God. In the unity of the Godhead there are three Persons, of one substance, power, and eternity—God the Father, God the Son, and God the Holy Ghost. The Father is one, neither begotten nor proceeding; the Son is eternally begotten of the Father; the Holy Ghost eternally proceeding from the Father and the Son." These church creeds continued to use the terms originally adopted by the church fathers. Although the terms "trinity" and "persons" were not found in the Scriptures, they did believe that they were adequate terms of communication to the people of their respective generations.

Contemporary evangelical theologians have chosen to retain those words and to explain them adequately for their twentieth century audiences. Loraine Boettner wrote: "The Father, Son, and Holy Spirit can be distinguished, but they cannot be separated; for they each possess the same identical numerical substance or essence. They do not merely exist alongside of each other, as did Washington, Jefferson, and Franklin, but they permeate and interpenetrate each other, are in and through each other." [2] He further stated: "What the one knows, the others know; what the one desires, the others desire; and what the one wills, the others will. Independence and self-existence are not attributes of the individual persons, but of the Triune God . . ." [3]

The difference between orthodoxy and heresy is often found in an understatement, overstatement, or misstatement, rather than in a blatant denial. Evangelicals should be cautious not to state more or less than what the Scriptures teach. Their choice of words should be purposeful.

Subordination

Did Jesus contradict Himself when He claimed before His enemies, "I and my Father are one" (John 10:30), and later before His disciples, ". . . my Father is greater than I" (John 14:28)? The answer is negative. Both statements are paradoxically true. Boettner explained: "This subordination of the Son to the Father, and of the Spirit to the Father and the Son, relates not to their essential life within the Godhead, but only to their modes of operation or their division of labour in creation and redemption." [4] This distinction has been called the difference between the ontological trinity and the economic trinity. The former deals with God as *He is* and the latter as *He acts*. The Father and the Son share the same divine essence, but the Father sent the Son. Both the Father and the Son sent the Spirit (John 14:26; 15:26).

Paul wrote: "But I would have you know, that the head of every man is Christ; and the head of the woman is the man; and the head of Christ is God" (1 Cor. 11:3). This is a functional, not an essential, headship. In Christ, "there is neither male nor female" (Gal. 3:28). Both are one in Him. Both share equally the essence of justification, sanctification, and glorification. The man is not greater or more saved than the woman. However, in the family and in the local church, there is authoritative order in order for those institutions to operate without conflict of interests. The same is true of the trinity. There is equality of the Persons; one is not more divine than the other. However, in the plan of redemption, there is authoritative order for the accomplishment of those purposes.

Denials of Trinitarianism

One segment of contemporary Pentecostalism is committed to modalistic trinitarianism. Commonly known as the "Jesus Only" group, they claim that God is not only one in essence but in Person as well. At one time, God revealed Himself as the Father; nineteen hundred years ago, He manifested Himself as the Son, and today He is in the mode of the Spirit. Thus, the names "Father, Son, and Spirit" are given to the three modes or manifestations in which God has revealed Himself. This view cannot adequately explain such verses as: "But when the Comforter is come, whom I will send unto you from the Father" (John 15:26). How could all three modes be in existence at the same time and yet all refer to the same Person?

The most vehement denial of the trinity comes from the sect called "Jehovah's Witnesses." Their sarcastic arguments stem from a complete misrepresentation of the orthodox doctrine of the trinity. For example, one wrote: "There are some clergymen, no doubt, who are really sincere in thinking that Jesus was his own Father, and the Almighty is the son of himself, and that each of these is a third person who is the same as the other two, and yet different from them." [5] No responsible trinitarian theologian ever taught that "Jesus was his own Father." The Witnesses have done exactly what the Athanasian Creed warned against; they have confounded the Persons and have accused the trinitarian of dividing the substance. In one of their propaganda booklets, the Witnesses paraphrased John 1:1 in three different ways, substituting for "God" first "the trinity," secondly "God the Father," and finally "God the Father and God the Holy Ghost." They then read the verse and showed how irrational all three versions sounded. How could the Word be the trinity? How could he be the Father? How could the Word be both the Father and the Spirit? They concluded: "Since we cannot scientifically calculate that 1 God (the Father) + 1 God (the Son) + 1 God (the Holy Ghost) = 1 God, then we must calculate that ⅓ God (the Father) + ⅓ God (The Son) ⅓ God (the Holy Ghost) = 3/3 God, or 1 God." [6] They argue that trinitarians must believe in the existence of three Gods or in the division of one God into three parts. This is purely a "straw man" argument. It is easy to disprove and to ridicule a position when that view is misunderstood or misrepresented.

Conclusion

Granted that God exists and that He exists in three eternal Persons, the incarnation becomes most plausible. J. V. Langmead Casserley, professor of Dogmatic Theology at the General Theological Seminary, candidly observed: "Whether or not we accept the Gospel narrative depends primarily on the Christological and philosophical presuppositions with which we approach it. From one point of view it [the virgin birth] may seem impossible, while from the other it appears to be the most natural thing in the world." [7] Atheism and unitarianism cannot maintain a literal incarnation of God within their systems. Their presuppositional foundations automatically rule out the entrance of God into the human race and into our time-space universe through the virgin birth.

In a different twist, Mikolaski argued: "Hence Christians test the truth of the doctrine of the Trinity by the truth of the doctrine of the Incarnation, and not vice versa." [8] If Jesus Christ is really God, then the virgin birth occurred; then the incarnation was real; then the nature of God must be trinitarian. This is a logical sequence.

2 The Question Of Messiah

Does the doctrine of the virgin birth simply imply that a human being was conceived within the womb of a woman apart from spermatic fertilization? Or, does it involve the entrance into this human world of a preexistent, nonhuman being? Did Jesus begin to exist within Mary's womb, or did He always exist? Was He merely an angel or a spirit creature who changed his mode of existence, or was He the eternal God the Son: Did Jesus possess deity or divinity? Some have defined "divinity" as the similarity of nature between Christ and God. This divinity, we are told, resides in all men because of man's spiritual resemblance to God; he was made in God's own image. These proponents would never speak about the "deity" in man unless they were committed to pantheism. However, Jesus possessed real deity, the identity or sameness of the essence of God. He was God; He was not just like God.

Messiah = God

In the first century, the rabbinical interpretation of the expectant Messiah was that he would be only human, the physical descendant of David. However, the Old Testament both intimated and clearly declared that He would be God as well as man. In his closing words to Israel, Moses predicted that Israel would be scattered among the nations for her sins and that after she repented: "That then the Lord thy God will turn thy captivity, and have compassion upon thee, and will return, and gather thee from all the nations . . ." (Deut. 30:3). The words *will return* involve a heaven-to-earth descent, an event that will be fulfilled in Christ's second advent after the great tribulation (cf. Matt. 24:27–31).

The Messiah was identified as "his [Jehovah's] anointed," "my king," "my Son," and perhaps as "Jehovah" by God Himself (Ps. 2:2, 6, 7, 11, 12). Another wrote of Him: "Thy throne, O God, is forever and ever: the sceptre of thy kingdom is a right sceptre" (Ps. 45:6). Here the future earthly king was equated with Elohim [God]. David testified: "The Lord [Jehovah] said unto my Lord [Adonai], Sit thou at my right hand, until I make thine enemies thy footstool" (Ps. 110:1). Jesus argued that the phrase "my Lord" meant that the Messiah would not only be the physical son of David, but that He would also be the Son of God or deity (Matt. 22:41–46). Why would David acknowledge his direct or distant son to be his Lord? No father worships his son. By the Spirit of God, David sensed that the Messiah would be God.

As written revelation increased, so did the prophetic concept that the Messiah would possess deity. Isaiah revealed to King Ahaz and to his royal house: "Therefore the Lord Himself shall give you a sign; Behold, a virgin shall conceive, and bear a son, and shall call his name Immanuel" (Isa. 7:14).[1] A supernatural sign, virgin conception, virgin birth, and the naming of a human child as "God with us" (Immanuel) are all linked together for the first time. How could a mere baby be God? The prophet later reinforced this idea: "For unto us a child is born, unto us a son is given: and the government shall be upon his shoulder: and his name shall be called Wonderful, Counsellor, The mighty God, The everlasting Father, The Prince of Peace" (Isa. 9:6). The dual nature of the Messiah is evident here. As a born child, He has a human nature; as a son given by God the Father, He has a divine nature. It is only because He is both divine and human that He could be rightfully called "the mighty God." No mere man could be named with the name of God nor would any man dare to usurp His name.

Jeremiah lucidly wrote:

Behold, the days come, saith the Lord, that I will raise unto David a righteous Branch, and a King shall reign and prosper, and shall execute judgment and justice in the earth.
In his days Judah shall be saved, and Israel shall dwell safely: and this is his name whereby he shall be called, THE LORD OUR RIGHTEOUSNESS (Jer. 23:5-6).

The Messiah would be a descendant of David, a king, a judge, a savior, and also God. Earlier, he identified Jehovah both as the "king of nations" and the "everlasting king" (Jer. 10:7, 10). Jehovah was not only to be their king, but also their redeemer. He was to save them from both their sins and their political enemies (Jer. 14:7–8; 50:34).

In his apocalyptic visions, Daniel reported:

> I saw in the night visions, and, behold, one like the Son of man came with the clouds of heaven, and came to the Ancient of days, and they brought him near before him.
> And there was given him dominion, and glory, and a kingdom, that all people, nations, and languages, should serve him: his dominion is an everlasting dominion, which shall not pass away, and his kingdom that which shall not be destroyed (Dan. 7:13-14).

Here the Messiah is identified as the Son of Man, a heavenly resident, the object of human worship and obedience, and the king of an everlasting kingdom. Since Jehovah was earlier called an everlasting king (Jer. 10:10), then the Son of Man must also share in the divine being. Only a trinitarian concept of God can solve this paradoxical, exegetical dilemma.

Micah, a contemporary of Isaiah, wrote this familiar verse: "But thou, Bethlehem Ephratah, though thou be little among the thousands of Judah, yet out of thee shall he come forth unto me that is to be ruler in Israel; whose goings forth have been from of old, from everlasting" (Micah 5:2). The paradox continues. The future king would be born in David's city of birth, but at the same time, He is an eternal personality. Only God is eternal, without beginning.

Zechariah spoke of the crucifixion of Jehovah. How could God suffer or die? Jehovah said: "And I will pour upon the house of David, and upon the inhabitants of Jerusalem, the spirit of Grace and of supplications: and they shall look upon me whom they have pierced . . ." (Zech. 12:10). In a messianic psalm, David quoted these words of the redeemer: ". . . they pierced my hands and my feet" (Ps. 22:16). In order for Jehovah to be pierced, He had to become a man to experience human suffering at the hands of men. God also said: "Awake, O sword, against my shepherd, and against the man that is my fellow, saith the Lord of hosts: smite the shepherd, and the sheep shall be scattered . . ."

(Zech. 13:7). How can a smitten man be the fellow of God? Only if that man was also God.

In one of the closing prophecies of the Old Testament, Malachi wrote: "Behold, I will send my messenger, and he shall prepare the way before me: and the Lord, whom ye seek, shall suddenly come to his temple, even the messenger of the covenant, whom ye delight in: behold, he shall come, saith the Lord of hosts" (Mal. 3:1). Here the Messiah is identified as the Lord, the owner of the temple, the messenger of the covenant, and the delight of Israel. Jehovah said that His own way would be prepared by a messenger, a reference to John the Baptist. Thus, Jehovah sends the Lord (Adonai), and yet the Lord is Jehovah. This is entirely harmonious with the oneness of God and the plurality of three Persons within the Godhead.

The Messiah was to be preceded by an anonymous messenger: "The voice of him that crieth in the wilderness, Prepare ye the way of the Lord [Jehovah], make straight in the desert a highway for our God" (Isa. 40:3). Jehovah was to come to earth to reign over a redeemed, restored Israel.

J. Barton Payne, professor of Old Testament at The Covenant Theological Seminary (St. Louis), provided this analysis of the "Messiah = Jehovah" concept: "Actually, the Old Testament itself so openly describes the Messiah in terms of deity, as sometimes to obliterate the line of demarcation between the Son of David and Yahweh God of Israel, and to produce what Warfield has called 'the coalescence of the advent of the Messiah and the advent of Jehovah.' " [2]

Messiah = God = Jesus Christ

The noted British New Testament scholar, F. F. Bruce, noted: "Fuller apprehension [of His Messiahship] followed his death and exaltation, however, and nothing is more eloquent in this regard than the spontaneous and unselfconscious way in which New Testament writers take Old Testament passages which refer to the God of Israel and apply them to Jesus, whom they all knew to be a real man." [3] According to the apostles and their associates, Jesus of Nazareth was not just a man; He was Jehovah God. In direct quotation and indirect allusion, their books are saturated with this identification.

Matthew saw in the virgin conception the entrance of Immanuel into the world of humanity (Matt. 1:23 cf. Isa. 7:14).

God said: "I, even I, am the Lord [Jehovah]; and beside me there is no saviour" (Isa. 43:11). Later, He added: "Look unto me, and be ye saved, all the ends of the earth: for I am God, and there is none else" (Isa. 45:22). Salvation was in Jehovah God, and yet, Jesus was the one who would save Israel from her sins (Matt. 1:21). The angels informed the shepherds: "For unto you is born this day in the city of David a Saviour, which is Christ the Lord" (Luke 2:11). Only in Christ can be found salvation "for there is none other name under heaven given among men, whereby we must be saved" (Acts 4:12 cf. John 3:16–17). Paul identified God as the Saviour (Titus 1:3; 3:4) and declared that Saviour-God to be Jesus Christ. In the Philippian prison, the jailor asked Paul and Silas: "Sirs, what must I do to be saved?" And they said, "Believe on the Lord Jesus Christ, and thou shalt be saved, and thy house" (Acts 16:30–31). Only if Jesus was God could He rightfully be called the object of saving faith. The Samaritans correctly named Christ "the Saviour of the World" (John 4:42). Simeon saw in the infant Jesus God's "salvation" (Luke 2:30).

God identified Himself as the Redeemer (Isa. 43:14; Hosea 13:14). Jesus was so considered by the priest Zacharias (Luke 1:68), by the prophetess Anna (Luke 2:38), by Paul (Gal. 3:13; Eph. 1:17), by Peter (1 Peter 1:18–19), and by the apocalyptic living creatures and the twenty-four elders (Rev. 5:9). No mere man can redeem his fellow man; only God can redeem the soul (Ps. 49:7–8 cf. 49:15). Thus, Jesus as the redeemer, must be God.

Jehovah claimed to be "the Holy One" (Isa. 43:15). He was so acknowledged by the angelic seraphim (Isa. 6:3). The angel Gabriel then announced to Mary that "that holy thing which shall be born of thee shall be called the Son of God" (Luke 1:35). The demons called Jesus of Nazareth "the Holy One of God" (Luke 4:34). In the first Christian sermon ever preached, Peter claimed that Jesus in His person and in His death and resurrection fulfilled the Davidic messianic psalm: "Because thou wilt not leave my soul in hell, neither wilt thou suffer thine Holy One to see corruption" (Acts 2:27 cf. 2:30–31; Ps. 16:10). Paul later made the same equation (Acts 13:35–39). No man, born in an ordinary way, could ever be called the Holy One. All men are born with an inherent sinful nature and soon manifest that tendency in their evil thoughts and deeds (Ps. 51:5; Rom. 3:9–18).

Jehovah regarded Himself as the King of Israel (Isa. 43:15). Concerning the millennial kingdom, Zechariah claimed: "And the Lord [Jehovah] shall be king over all the earth: in that day shall there be one Lord, and his name one" (Zech. 14:9 cf. 14:16). Earlier, it was predicted that the King would come to Jerusalem riding upon an ass (Zech. 9:9). All of the Gospel writers agreed with Matthew when he wrote concerning the triumphal entry of Jesus: "All this was done, that it might be fulfilled, which was spoken by the prophet, saying" (Matt. 21:4 cf. Zech. 9:9). The climax of the Biblical prophetic program is the return of Jesus Christ to the earth and the subsequent establishment of His reign. In describing His advent, John wrote: "And he hath on his vesture and on his thigh a name written, "KING OF KINGS, AND LORD OF LORDS" (Rev. 19:16). As *the* King, Jesus must also be God.

The opening commandments marked out God as the only object of human worship, and obedience (Ex. 20:1–6). When Satan wanted Jesus to fall down and worship him, Christ refused and quoted the law: "Thou shalt worship the Lord thy God, and him only shalt thou serve" (Matt. 4:10 cf. Deut. 6:13). And yet, Hebrews charged: "And again, when he bringeth in the firstbegotten into the world, he saith, And let all the angels of God worship him" (Heb. 1:6). When Lucifer (Satan) wanted to be worshipped as God by his fellow angels, he fell from his high estate, and yet, God here commanded the angels to worship Christ. Angels were only to praise Jehovah (Ps. 148:2). Christ therefore must not be an exalted angelic or human creature, but God the Son. God also said: "That unto me every knee shall bow, every tongue shall swear" (Isa. 45:23). This reference was used by Paul to show that all believers would bow at the judgment seat of Christ (Rom. 14:10–12) and that all men would bow before Him in eternity:

Wherefore God also hath highly exalted him, and given him a name which is above every name:

That at the name of Jesus every knee should bow, of things in heaven, and things in earth, and things under the earth;

And that every tongue should confess that Jesus Christ is Lord to the glory of God the Father (Phil. 2:9–11).

Later, it will be shown that Jesus did not refuse worship of Himself either before or after His death and resurrection. Only God should be worshipped; therefore, the Biblical authors regarded Him as God.

Isaiah asserted that "the everlasting God, the Lord [Jehovah]" was "the Creator of the ends of the earth" (Isa. 40:28). The creation of the material universe was ascribed to Jesus by both John (John 1:3) and Paul (Col. 1:16).

Both David (Ps. 18:2) and Hannah (1 Sam. 2:2) acknowledged Jehovah to be their Rock, their strength. Paul claimed that the smiting of a literal rock in the wilderness by Moses was a type or picture of the crucifixion of Christ, the spiritual Rock of the believer (1 Cor. 10:4 cf Ex. 17:6). Peter called Him "a rock of offence" and the "chief corner stone" (1 Peter 2:6–8).

Throughout the Old Testament times, saints addressed their prayers to God, never to angels or to men. The Spirit-filled Stephen, at his martyrdom prayed a double petition: "Lord Jesus, receive my spirit" and "Lord, lay not this sin to their charge" (Acts 7:59–60).

When Simeon saw the baby Jesus, by the Spirit of God, he identified Him with this Biblical quotation: "A light to lighten the Gentiles, and the glory of thy people Israel" (Luke 2:32 cf. Isa. 42:6). Isaiah described Jehovah as "an everlasting light," one who would make the sun, moon, and stars obsolete (Isa. 60:19–20). In the eternal city, the Lamb (Christ) will provide its light (Rev. 21:23).

The being of God is glorious. He Himself said: "I am the Lord [Jehovah]: that is my name: and my glory will I not give to another" (Isa. 42:8). Earlier, Isaiah had seen a vision of God in all His glory and holiness (Isa. 6:1–4). The apostle John later commented: "These things said Isaiah, when he saw his glory, and spake of Him" (John 12:41). John was here referring to the person of Jesus Christ.

Concerning the last days of Israel, Joel declared: "And it shall come to pass, that whosoever shall call on the name of the Lord [Jehovah] shall be delivered . . ." (Joel 2:32). In his Pentecostal sermon, Peter quoted that verse and identified "the Lord" as Jesus Christ (Acts 2:21 cf. 2:22, 25, 34, 36, 38). Paul likewise wrote that men must "confess with the mouth the Lord Jesus" and must "call upon the name of the Lord Jesus" in order to be spiritually saved (Rom. 10:9, 13).

Ezekiel stated that the voice of the God of Israel was "like a noise of many waters" (Ezek. 43:2), the same expression ascribed to the voice of the resurrected Christ by John (Rev. 1:15).

All Biblical writers agree that John the Baptist was the fulfillment of the prophecy concerning the forerunner of the Messiah: "The voice of him that crieth in the wilderness, Prepare ye the way of the Lord [Jehovah], make straight in the desert a highway for our God" (Isa. 40:3 cf. Luke 3:4). Since John actually prepared the way for Jesus Christ and pointed his disciples toward Him, therefore both John and the Gospel authors must have recognized Jesus to be "the Lord [Jehovah]" mentioned by Isaiah.

The eternity and the immutability of God were clearly expressed by the Psalmist: "They [earth and heavens] shall perish, but thou shalt endure: yea, all of them shall wax old like a garment; as a vesture shalt thou change them, and they shall be changed. But thou art the same, and thy years shall have no end" (Ps. 102:25–27). In order to show the superiority of Jesus Christ to the angels, the author of Hebrews quoted these verses as references to Christ (Heb. 1:10–12). He also claimed that Jesus Christ was "the same yesterday, and today, and forever" (Heb. 13:8). Since "all flesh is as grass, and all the glory of man as the flower of grass" (1 Peter 1:24), then Christ was not regarded as a mere man. God Himself said: "For I am the Lord [Jehovah], I change not" (Mal. 3:6). An unchangeable Christ must also be the immutable Jehovah.

In expounding upon the physical ascension of Christ into heaven, His exaltation over the church, and the giving of spiritual gifts to church leaders, Paul quoted a passage from a psalm that attributed the ascension to God Himself (Eph. 4:8–10 cf. Ps. 68:17–18).

One name of God is "THE LORD OUR RIGHTEOUSNESS" (Jer. 23:6). Only God is righteous in Himself; only He is the source of righteousness; only He can make a repentant sinner righteous. The acceptance of a believer by God is found in his spiritual position in Christ. Paul wrote: "But of him are ye in Christ Jesus, who of God is made unto us . . . righteousness" (1 Cor. 1:30 cf. Eph. 1:6). How could a person be made righteous in one who himself was not divinely righteous?

Jehovah knew that one day He would be pierced (Zech. 12:10). When the body of Jesus was pierced on the cross but his bones were left unbroken, John, who witnessed the events, claimed that the fulfillment of Zechariah's prophecy had occurred (John 19:31–37). John later reaffirmed this fact (Rev. 1:7).

It is clear that the New Testament authors equated Jehovah with Jesus. Critics can doubt their conclusion, but they cannot doubt the fact that the writers so regarded Jesus.

3

The Claims
Of the Apostles

Not only did the Biblical writers apply Old Testament passages concerning Jehovah God to the person of Jesus Christ, but they also directly attributed deity to Him. They named Him as God and ascribed to Him both divine attributes and activities.

John opened his Gospel: "In the beginning was the Word, and the Word was with God, and the Word was God" (John 1:1). The language seems clear enough, and yet there is much exegetical controversy about this verse. The Jehovah's Witnesses in their *New World Translation* translate the third phrase: "and the Word was a god." They point out that the definite article does not appear before the word "God" in the third phrase; therefore, the indefinite article "a" must be supplied. The actual Greek text reads: *en archei en ho logos, kai ho logos en pros ton theon, kai theos en ho logos.* The definite article *ho* appears before the Greek word for "Word" in all three usages. The article appears before the word for "God" in the second phrase, but not in the third. The observation of the Witnesses is correct, but their translation is grammatically wrong. Ernest Cadman Colwell, professor of Greek at the University of Chicago, concluded in his study of the Greek article: "A definite predicate nominative has the article when it follows the verb; it does not have the article when it precedes the verb." [1] The *New World Translation* listed thirty-five passages to show why "a" should be included, but in every case the predicate noun stood after the verb. In this sentence, "the word" stands as the subject of the verb; "was" is the verb; and "God" is the predicate nominative. John is predicating to the person of the Word (Christ) the quality of the Word "God." All that *theos* means, the Word was that in the beginning. Since the word *theos* ("God") is a noun, it would be wrong to say that the Word was divine or God-like; these terms are adjectives. A parallel construction was later used by John: "God is love" (1 John 4:8). The Greek text reads *ho theos agape estin*. It would be just as wrong to say "God is *a* love" as to state "God is loving or lovely." God is love. Whatever the word "love" connotes, God is that. To say "the Word is a god" is to misunderstand Greek grammar. The Greek has no word for the indefinite English articles "a" or "an." The absence of the definite article designates that the quality of the noun is being emphasized. The fact that the predicate nominative *theos* stands before the verb in the third clause shows that John was emphasizing the deity of the Word: "and *God* was the Word." Actually, if the definite article had appeared before *theos,* the trinitarian concept would have been absolutely destroyed. If *the* Word was before *the* God, how could *the* Word also be *the* God? This would mean that the Father and the Son would be the same Person. The reason why the article appears before God in the second clause is to show the distinction of persons between the Word (Son) and the God (Father). The reason for its omission in the third clause is to reveal that the Word was God without being the Father. The only way that this could be so would be if there was a plurality of Persons within the Godhead. Actually, the Witnesses are most inconsistent in their translation. The article does not appear later before *theos* (John 1:12, 13, 18), but they don't translate those usages "a god." This argument should be pressed further. John wrote: "No man hath seen God at any time . . ." (John 1:18). Since the article does not appear, according to them, it should be translated: "no man hath seen *a* god at any time." Since they earlier identified the Word (Jesus) as a god, did not people see Him? Their position becomes historically and grammatically ridiculous. The use of the verb "was" is also significant. It marks uncreated being. The Word was God; He did not become God at any point of time. He came to be man (John 1:14). The verb "was made" is *egeneto*, the same word translated for the appearance of John the Baptist (1:6—"was"). John came to be; he did not always exist.

When the doubter Thomas was challenged by the resurrected Christ to touch Him, the apostle "said unto him, My Lord and My

God" (John 20:28). The Witnesses claim that Thomas looked horizontally at Jesus and said "My Lord" and then lifted his head vertically toward the heavenly Father and remarked "My God." However, the passage nowhere substantiates this claim for double addressees. Thomas said *to him,* not *to them,* or *to him* and *to him.* Thomas acknowledged Jesus as his human messiah ("My Lord") and as his God ("My God"). John wanted his readers to acknowledge the same two truths (20:30–31). In his mind, the phrases "my Lord" and "the Christ" were identical and so also were the titles "my God" and "the Son of God." Christ did not rebuke Thomas for his worship or identification; rather He claimed that he was blessed for doing so.

Speaking of Israel, Paul wrote: "Whose are the fathers, and of whom as concerning the flesh Christ came, who is over all, God blessed forever" (Rom. 9:5). Here the apostle identified Christ not only as a Jewish human being but also as the sovereign God. The *Revised Standard Version,* however, created a furor with this translation of the verse: "to them belong the patriarchs, and of their race, according to the flesh, is the Christ. God who is over all be blessed forever." Here Christ is only described in His humanity. The blessing upon God is upon the Father, thus the RSV does not see this verse as a claim for Christ's deity by Paul. However, the RSV did carry this footnote on the verse: "Or *Christ, who is God over all, blessed for ever."* There were no marks of punctuation in the original Greek text, thus the arbitrary placement of commas by translators definitely reflects their Christological presuppositions. The grammatical position of the words seems to favor the AV reading.

Paul argued that his apostleship was "not of men, neither by man, but by Jesus Christ, and God the Father, who raised him from the dead" (Gal. 1:1). He claimed divine, not human, origin for his ministerial office. This does not mean that Paul rejected the humanity of Christ; rather he knew Christ to be more than a mere man. Thus, He had to be either an angel or God. The latter was Paul's view.

In the famous kenosis passage, the apostle claimed that Christ in eternity past was "being [existing] in the form of God" (Phil. 2:6). He further stated that He was "equal with God" (Phil.

2:6). These two expressions show that all that God was, Christ was. When the Jews charged Jesus with blasphemy for "making himself equal with God" (John 5:18), they used the same word for equality (*ison*) that Paul employed here (*isa*). Equality with God meant a sameness of essence, not a similarity of attitude or action. The latter is to be commended and encouraged among men, not to be condemned.

Paul described the believer's expectation thusly: "Looking for that blessed hope, and the glorious appearing of the great God and our Saviour Jesus Christ" (Titus 2:13). The question is obvious: Is Christ not only Savior, but also the great God? The answer comes from both eschatology (doctrine that deals with future events) and Greek grammar. Nowhere in the New Testament is the believer instructed to look for the coming of God the Father; however, constantly he is admonished to await the advent of the Son, even Jesus Christ (John 14:1–3; 1 Thess. 1:10). In the Greek text, the closing words read: *tou megalou theou kai soteros hemon Jesou Christou*. The definite article *tou* appears before the word *theou* (God) but not before *soteros* (Savior). The famous grammarian, Granville Sharp, recognized this rule: "When the copulative *kai* connects two nouns of the same case, if the article *ho* or any of its cases precedes the first of the said nouns or participles, and is not repeated before the second noun or participle, the latter always relates to the same person that is expressed or described by the first noun or participle; i.e., it denotes a further description of the first-named person." [2] Thus, "God" is clearly identified as Jesus Christ. The same type of literary construction is used by Peter to support the deity of Christ (2 Peter 1:1; 2:20).

John ended his First Epistle: ". . . and we are in him that is true, even in his Son Jesus Christ. This is the true God, and eternal life" (1 John 5:20). The problem concerns the grammatical antecedent of the demonstrative pronoun "this." Does it refer to the Father ("the true one" cf. "his") or to the Son, Jesus Christ? Grammatically, it could go either way. John, however, was pointing to Christ. Earlier the apostle entitled Christ "that eternal life, which was with the Father and was manifested unto us" (1 John 1:2). Just as the Word was with *the* God (John 1:1) so the eternal life was with the Father (1 John 1:2 cf. John 1:4; 14:6). John is here describing a single person who is known both as the true God and eternal life. The Granville Sharp rule applies here also because the definite article appears before "God" but not before "life." Christ is that Person.

The New Testament saints not only named Jesus Christ as God, but they also ascribed to Him attributes that are rightfully only the prerogatives of God Almighty. They saw Him as having existence before His birth or incarnation. Even though John the Baptist was six months older than Jesus he stated: "He that cometh after me is preferred before me: for he was before me" (John 1:15). The phrase "before me" definitely denotes preexistence and may imply eternality. The apostle John claimed that in such a time that could be called "beginning," Jesus already was existing (John 1:2). Only an eternal God could exist before the beginning. God never began to be; but all that is non-God did. Christ was "before all things" (Col. 1:17). He was not a "thing" Himself, but before things came to be, He was already existing. Hebrews states of Him: "Thy throne, O God, is forever and ever" (Heb. 1:8). If He has an eternal throne, then He must be eternal to sit upon it.

With God there "is no variableness, neither shadow of turning" (James 1:17). He is constant, unchanging, immutable. Of Christ one wrote: ". . . the same yesterday, and today, and forever" (Heb. 13:8). Men are as unstable as the sun-withered grass (1 Peter 1:24), thus the sameness of Christ must manifest His divine nature (cf. Heb. 1:10–12).

John claimed that Jesus "knew all men, and needed not that any should testify of man: for he knew what was in man" (John 2:24–25). Some might attempt to explain Jesus as clairvoyant or as a master psychologist; however, this verse conveys more than extraordinary human insight. It is an axiom that "man looketh on the outward appearance, but the Lord looketh on the heart" (1 Sam. 16:7). Peter admitted to the resurrected Christ: "Lord, thou knowest all things" (John 21:17). He appealed to Christ's omniscience as the support for his moral integrity. Earlier the entire group of apostles affirmed this truth (John 16:30). Paul wrote: "In whom [Christ] are hid all the treasures of wisdom and knowledge" (Col. 2:3). No finite mind can contain or understand the totality of divine omniscience.

To the apostles, Christ was omnipotent. Paul said that Christ "shall change our vile body, that it may be fashioned like unto his glorious body, according to the working whereby he is able even to subdue all things unto himself" (Phil. 3:21). Only God can frame a body out of decomposed human dust. Creation is an expression of omnipotence. To the Biblical writers, Christ was the Creator. John wrote: "All things were made by him [Christ]; and without him was not anything made that was made" (John 1:3). Later he added: "He was in the world, and the world was made by him" (John 1:10). Some claim that Christ was only the agent of creation because of the usage of the preposition "by" [*dia*]. Their concept is that God created the world through Jesus and that Christ did not exercise an innate omnipotence. However, the same preposition is used for the Father's work in creation (Rom. 11:36). Paul claimed: "For by him [Christ] were all things created, that are in heaven, and that are in earth, visible and invisible, whether they be thrones, or dominions, or principalities, or powers: all things were created by him, and for him" (Col. 1:16). In addition, the writers asserted that Christ maintains what He created. Paul wrote: ". . . and by him all things consist" (Col. 1:17). Another said that Christ upholds "all things by the word of his power" (Heb. 1:3). The disciples knew nothing of "Mother nature." What modern man labels "natural law," they attributed to the sustaining power of Christ.

If Christ were only a creature (man or angel) how could He be in more than one place at one time? In His resurrected human body, He is today in the third heaven, the very presence of the Father (Acts 1:9–11; 7:56; 1 Thess. 1:10; 4:16), and yet in His spiritual omnipresence, He can indwell every believer (Gal. 2:20; Col. 1:27). It is the nature of God to be everywhere present in the totality of His being (Ps. 139:7–10). It is correct to say that God is both here and there. God can't be divided; therefore it is wrong to say that God is here and not there or to say that part of God is here and part of God is there. Since Christ partakes of the nature of God, He also can be everywhere present in the totality of His divine being. At the same time, since He joined Himself to a human body, it is right to say that He is in heaven, and not on earth today. This refers to His local or manifested presence. This paradox could only be true of one who is Himself God.

To them, Christ was holy. He was "holy, harmless, undefiled, separate from sinners" (Heb. 7:26). Paul stated that although Christ was made to be sin for believers, He "knew no sin" (2 Cor. 5:21). Peter added that the moral character of Him was "without blemish and without spot" (1 Peter 1:19). This could never be said of or by any mortal man (cf. Rom. 3:9–19). The person who claims to be sinless is either self-deceived or a liar or both (1 John 1:8–10). Those who claim such moral virtue for another human being are also deluded.

When Abraham was informed by Jehovah about the imminent destruction of Sodom and Gomorrah, he made this appeal: "Shall not the Judge of all the earth do right?" (Gen. 18:25). The apostles later identified Jesus Christ as that judge. Peter declared to the Roman centurion Cornelius that it was Jesus who "was ordained of God to be the Judge of quick [living peoples] and dead" (Acts 10:42). Paul told the pagan philosophers of Athens that God had "appointed a day, in the which he will judge the world in righteousness by that man whom he hath ordained" (Acts 17:31). Later to Timothy he wrote: "I charge thee therefore before God, and the Lord Jesus Christ, who shall judge the quick and the dead at his appearing and his kingdom" (2 Tim. 4:1).

Paul opened all of his epistles with this type of invocation: "Grace to you and peace from God our Father and the Lord Jesus Christ" (Rom. 1:7 cf. 1 Cor. 1:2; 2 Cor. 1:2; Gal. 1:3; Eph. 1:2; Phil. 1:2; Col. 1:2; 1 Thess. 1:1; 2 Thess. 1:2; 1 Tim. 1:2; 2 Tim. 1:2; Titus 1:4; Philem. v. 3). Daily, sustaining grace and peace had a double source. How could a creature, human or angelic, be linked with God as the originators of such blessings? Paul could have never said: "Grace and peace from God and from Michael or Gabriel." Nor could he have written: "Grace and peace from God and from me or Timothy or Peter." In Paul's mind, Christ was the equal of the Father.

There is a subtle reference to Christ's deity in the Pauline affirmation: "For there is one God, and one mediator between God and men, the man Christ Jesus" (1 Tim. 2:5). A mediator must be the equal of the two parties between whom he mediates. Thus, in order to represent man, he must be human, and in order to represent God, he must also be divine. There can only be one mediator; therefore, he must be one person with two natures.

Concerning the first advent of Christ, John wrote: "For this purpose the Son of God was manifested, that he might destroy the works of the devil" (1 John 3:8). Nowhere is it stated that a created being was revealed or manifested. Only God has the ability to disclose Himself.

The attitude of the apostles toward the person of Jesus Christ can be summarized in this verse: "For in him dwelleth all the fulness of the Godhead bodily" (Col. 2:9). They knew Him to be a man, and yet they knew that the personality who tabernacled in that body was divine. To them, He was God manifest in the flesh. A relevant question is clear: How did He get to be that way? They did not believe that Jesus, a mere man, came to be God. Rather, they believed that God the Son became man and yet remained divine. What was the method for such an incarnation? As we shall see, the only adequate answer is the virgin conception under the providential control of the Holy Spirit.

4 Claims Made By Christ

Did the apostles make claims about Christ that He never made for Himself? If so, they could be charged with sincere, but overzealous exaggeration. In a sense, they would then be trying to develop a legend in their own generation. However, this was not the case. Their statements did not originate within their own theological intuition nor from a consensus of church opinion. They simply stated what Christ Himself said, applying and amplifying those concepts under the superintendence of the Spirit for various audiences.

He claimed to be the Jehovah God of the Old Testament. During a controversial dialogue, the Jews asked Him: "Thou art not yet fifty years old, and hast thou seen Abraham?" (John 8:57). In reply, Jesus answered: "Verily, verily, I say unto you, Before Abraham was, I am" (John 8:58). The Jews then almost stoned Him to death because in their opinion He had committed blasphemy by claiming to be the eternal God. Why did they react so violently? The Greek text reads *prin Abraam genesthai ego eimi* (literally: "Before Abraham came to be, I am"). If Jesus were merely asserting His preexistence (which would have been true for any angelic creature speaking), He would have only needed to say: "Before Abraham was, I was" or "Before Abraham came to be, I came to be." Christ not only contrasted two different verbs (*ginomai* and *eimi*), but also two different verbal tenses (the aorist infinitive *genesthai* and the present indicative *eimi*). The fact that He said "I am" meant that He was claiming for Himself the very name that God gave to Moses when He spoke to Moses out of the burning bush:

And Moses said unto God, Behold, when I come unto the children of Israel, and shall say unto them, The God of your fathers hath sent me unto you; and they shall say to me, What is his name? what shall I say unto them?

And God said unto Moses, I AM THAT I AM: and he said, Thus shalt thou say unto the children of Israel, I AM hath sent me unto you (Ex. 3:13-14).

The Hebrew word for Jehovah is based upon the Hebrew verb "to be" (hwh) with the addition of "y" (yhwh = Yahweh = Jehovah). The Hebrew text uses the first person singular verb *ahwh* ("I am"). The Greek equivalent is *ego eimi*, the same words used by Jesus. Christ reinforced the "I am" concept on several occasions by adding predicate nominatives. He said: "I am the bread of life" (John 6:35); "I am the light of the world" (John 8:12, 9:5); "I am the door" (John 10:7); "I am the good shepherd" (John 10:11, 14); "I am the resurrection and the life" (John 11:25); "I am the way, the truth, and the life" (John 14:6); and "I am the true vine" (John 15:1). How could Jesus claim to be the eternal "I am" and yet be less than fifty human years old? Where did He get this body that shows some degree of age? The answer can only lie in a normal birth procedure with one major exception: no paternal father.

On another occasion, Jesus asserted: "I and my Father are one" (John 10:30). Just before that claim, He had said that no one was able to pluck a believer out of His hands or out of His Father's hands (John 10:28–29). When the Jews were about to stone Him, He asked for their reason for doing so. They replied: "For a good work we stone thee not; but for blasphemy; and because that thou, being a man, makest thyself God" (John 10:33). Some have suggested that the oneness which Jesus mentioned referred only to the desire and the ability to keep the believer. However, if this were so, why did the Jews find fault with His statement? Would this not be a noble, good work? They may have questioned His ability to keep, but they would have commended his desire to do so. In order to have the same ability to keep as the Father, one must have the same power. Since God is omnipotent, then Christ must have been claiming almighty power for Himself. The Greek text reads *ego kai ho pater hen esmer* (literally; "I and the Father one we are"). In our way of thinking, Jesus did not use the expected preferential order: "The Father and I." In the Godhead, they are equal Persons, so any order of listing is perfectly acceptable. The phrase "one we are" refers to the oneness of the divine essence which they shared equally. Christ later argued.

Jesus answered them, Is it not written in your law, I said, Ye are gods?

If he called them gods, unto whom the word of God came, and the scripture cannot be broken;

Say ye of him, whom the Father hath sanctified, and sent into the world, Thou blasphemest; because I said, I am the Son of God? (John 10:34-36).

He argued from the less to the greater. When Old Testament prophets spoke in the name of God what God told them to speak, they figuratively became "gods" or "God" to their congregations. The attitude of the people toward them manifested their response toward God. Some have argued that Christ only claimed to be God or the Son of God in this sense. However, none of those Old Testament prophets in their preaching ever claimed to be equal with God, to be one with God. Herein lies the inseparable difference; Jesus did, but they didn't. That is why when Jesus added, "the Father is in me, and I in him" (John 10:38), they again tried to apprehend Him.

The expression "my Father" must be considered. Jesus addressed God as "Father" (John 17:1), "Holy Father" (John 17:11), and "my Father" (John 5:17). Never in His own prayers did He say "Our Father." When the disciples asked to be taught about prayer, He said unto them: "When *ye* pray, say, Our Father which art in heaven" (Luke 11:2). Jesus did not regard God to be the Father of the disciples in the same sense in which He was the Father of Himself. In His first postresurrection appearance, He told Mary Magdalene: ". . . go to my brethren, and say unto them, I ascend unto my Father, and your Father; and to my God, and your God" (John 20:17). Christ called them *"my* brethren," but He did not say "our Father" or "our God." His relationship to them as the offspring of Mary was one thing, but the relationship of them and of Him to God was altogether different. One reason why the Jews wanted to kill Him was because He said: "My Father worketh hitherto, and I work" (John 5:17). To them, "he not only had broken the sabbath, but said also that God was his Father, making himself equal with God" (John 5:18). What was wrong in calling God "Father"? There was nothing theologically improper in making such a declaration, but His wording startled and angered them. The usage of "my" was possessive. They accused Christ of calling God His own Father. The word "his" was not the common personal pronoun *autou*, but rather *idion*. To them, Christ was making a unique claim upon the fatherhood of God. He was the Father of Christ in a manner in which He was not the Father of anyone else.

Christ also claimed for Himself the attributes or prerogatives of deity. He claimed to exist before His human conception. He often used the verbal phrase "I am come" to denote His entrance into the world from a life of existence outside of this present time-space universe. He said that He had come to fulfill the law not to destroy it (Matt. 5:17), to send a sword not peace (Matt. 10:34), to preach (Mark 1:38), to call sinners to repentance (Mark 2:17), to minister and to give his life a ransom for many (Mark 10:45), to seek and to save that which was lost (Luke 19:10), to judge the world (John 9:39), and to bear witness unto the truth (John 18:37). He also claimed to exist before the world began. In His intercessory prayer uttered on the night before His crucifixion, He petitioned the Father: ". . . glorify thou me with thine own self with the glory which I had with thee before the world began" (John 17:5). He stated that the Father loved Him before the foundation of the world (John 17:24). He claimed that He had been in heaven before His earthly existence (John 3:13; [1] 6:33, 42, 50–51, 58, 62). He further asserted that the Father had sent Him into the world from heaven (John 7:16, 27–29, 33–34; 8:18, 26, 42; 16:28; 17:18). He constantly affirmed that He (His origin) was not of this world (John 8:23; 17:14). He startled Pilate by saying that His kingdom was not of this world (John 18:36). He claimed to be the eternal "I am" (John 8:58). In His final postresurrection appearance, sixty years after His ascension into heaven, He told the apostle John: "I am Alpha and Omega, the beginning and the end, the first and the last" (Rev. 22:13 cf. 1:8). Christ never perceived Himself to be just a thirty-three-year-old man; He was fully conscious of His eternal existence. From this fact, it is logical to assume that He was also aware of His means of entrance into the world. Vladimer Zaitsev, a Russian professor, speculated that Christ was a cosmonaut and that the star of Bethlehem was really a space ship that brought Him from an unidentified planet where justice and equality prevailed.[2] A more suitable explanation is that He knew that He was virgin born, not because Mary had told Him, but because He as the eternal God the Son was actively participating in the incarnation event. Although some rabbinical literature spoke about a heavenly preexistence for the Messiah,[3] the first century Jews completely repudiated Christ's claim to a heavenly descent.

Christ also predicated to Himself the attribute of omnipresence. During His earthly ministry, He assured His disciples: "For where two or three are gathered together in my name, there am I in the midst of them" (Matt. 18:20). He did not say that the spirit of His teaching would be there, nor that He would be in their presence by way of God's Spirit; rather, *He* personally would be there. The point that convinced Nathanael of Jesus' messiahship was the latter's declaration: "Before that Philip called thee, when thou wast under the fig tree, I saw thee" (John 1:48). Jesus did not have human eyes with Superman's capacity of X-ray vision. It does not appear that He was exercising His attribute of omniscience; otherwise, He would have said: "I knew that you were there." Christ *saw* him, although he was hidden from normal human vision. Christ saw him because He was there in His divine, spiritual omnipresence. Although God the Son was locally present in a human body, it should not be stated that He was no longer omnipresent. The human body was not ubiquitious (everwhere present), however. The Gospel of John records: "And no man hath ascended up to heaven, but he that came down from heaven, even the Son of man which is in heaven" (John 3:13). This verse, especially the last phrase, has puzzled both translators and exegetes. Was it spoken by Christ or was it an editorial comment added by John? If spoken by Christ, how could He say that He was still in heaven when He was right there speaking to Nicodemus? The only valid explanation from that approach is to say that Christ was referring to His spiritual omnipresence in heaven. Some ancient Greek manuscripts omit the last phrase, "even the

Son of man which is in heaven." Some textual critics believe that Christ spoke the content of the first part of the verse, but that scribes later interpolated the latter phrase to show their belief in the bodily presence of Christ in heaven. If the Authorized Version reading is correct, then it is best to conclude that John's editorial remarks began at that point and that Christ's conversation ended with the prior verse (3:12). Thus, when John wrote the Gospel, Christ had already been in heaven for over sixty years. The death and resurrection of Christ did not change the human qualities of His new materialistic body. Today, that body is in heaven at the right hand of the Father (Mark 16:19). Nevertheless, Jesus in His postresurrection commission to the apostles, stated: ". . . and, lo, I am with you alway, even unto the end of the world [age]" (Matt. 28:20). How can Jesus be in two places (heaven and earth) at the same time? Today, His manifested or local presence is in the third heaven (in the resurrection body), but since He is God, He can exercise His divine attribute of omnipresence by being on earth with Christians. God manifested Himself in Old Testament times in the cloud of His presence in the wilderness wanderings and in the Holy of Holies, the inner sanctuary of both the Mosaic tabernacle and the Solomonic temple, and yet, He still filled the universe with His omnipresence. Christ made the same claim for Himself.

Jesus claimed also to be omniscient. At the conclusion of His sermon on the bread of life, He declared: "But there are some of you that believe not" (John 6:64a). John further explained: "For Jesus knew from the beginning who they were that believed not, and who should betray him" (John 6 :64b). How did He know? The multitude had not openly manifested its unbelief before. None of the apostles knew that Judas was the traitor nor did Judas reveal his spiritual condition to anyone. Was Jesus simply a good student of human psychology, or did He manifest His capacity to look into the hearts of men (cf. Heb. 4:13)? He had complete knowledge of the events surrounding His death before they occurred: the hour of departure from the world (John 13:1), the traitor (John 13:11), the arrest and subsequent trials (John 18:4), and the fulfillment of Scripture in His sufferings (John 19:28). He once publicly proclaimed: "All things are delivered unto me of my Father: and·no man knoweth the Son, but the Father; neither knoweth any man the Father, save the Son, and he to whomsoever the Son will reveal him" (Matt. 11:27). How could He audaciously claim an exclusive knowledge of the Person of the Father? In fact, how could anyone know God except God Himself? Paul commented that "the things of God knoweth no man, but the Spirit of God" (1 Cor. 2:10). Jesus and Paul did not contradict each other even though the former omitted any reference to the Spirit and the latter omitted the Son. Jesus simply was emphasizing His relationship to the Father, whereas Paul was stressing the pivotal, teaching ministry of the Holy Spirit in the lives of believers. In both passages, the point is obvious: only God can know God and only God can reveal God to man. In His post-resurrection ministry, He declared to the church at Thyatira through John: ". . . I am he which searcheth the reins and hearts" (Rev. 2:23). Only God can actually do that (cf. 1 Sam. 16:7). When Jesus was twelve years old, Mary and Joseph accidentally left Him behind in Jerusalem when they embarked on a return trip to Nazareth. When they discovered their error, they later "found him in the temple, sitting in the midst of the doctors, both hearing them, and asking them questions. And all that heard him were astonished at his understanding and answers" (Luke 2:46–47). Some evangelicals have seen in this experience an expression of omniscience. However, it is better to conclude that Jesus manifested a knowledge, gained from a keen study of the Old Testament and an observation of human life, that was unmarred because of the absence of a sin nature. The world has known its share of child geniuses, and yet even these children lived purposeless moments and yielded to the pressures of sin. Luke later reported that "Jesus increased in wisdom" (Luke 2:52). The knowledge that Jesus displayed here as a youth and later in His sermons probably reflected a human intellect fully controlled by the Holy Spirit rather than an expression of omniscience.

Christ also claimed to be omnipotent. He stated: ". . . for the works which the Father hath given me to finish, the same works that I do, bear witness of me, that the Father hath sent me" (John 5:36). Later, when He was charged with the sin of blasphemy, He retorted: "If I do not the works of my Father, believe me not. But if I do, though ye believe not me, believe the works: that ye may know, and believe, that the Father is in me, and I in Him" (John 10:37–38). He constantly pointed to His miracles to support His claims. He cleansed the lepers, healed the palsied, removed fevers, calmed the stormy winds and the turbulent seas, cast out demons, raised the dead, restored sight to the blind, hearing to the deaf, and speech to the dumb, strengthened the lame, turned water into wine, multiplied the bread and the fish, and walked on the Sea of Galilee. Some have argued that in His performance of miracles, Christ was no different than the prophets or the apostles. They were able to do similar works because God either gave them the ability to do them or else worked through them. However, in spite of the similarities, there are some basic differences. The apostles never professed to do miracles in their own name. To the lame man at the Beautiful gate of the temple, Peter and John commanded: "In the name of Jesus Christ of Nazareth rise up and walk" (Acts 3:6). Later, in his explanatory sermon, Peter remarked: "Ye men of Israel, why marvel ye at this? or why look ye so earnestly on us, as though by our own power or holiness we had made this man to walk?" (Acts 3:12 cf. 4:10). To the palsied Aeneas, Peter said: "Jesus Christ maketh thee whole: arise, and make thy bed" (Acts 9:34). Barnabas and Paul were repulsed when suddenly they were acknowledged to be gods by the pagans because they had performed a miracle (Acts 14: 8–18). Jesus, however, willingly received worship after He had performed a miracle (Matt. 14:33). Jesus also claimed that the power to heal came from Him as the original source. To the blind men, He asked: "Believe me that I am able to do this?" (Matt. 9:28). When the woman who had a blood disease for twelve years touched His garment and was healed, Jesus said: "Somebody hath touched me: for I perceive that virtue is gone out of me" (Luke 8:46). In his excellent book on Christian apologetics, John Gerstner, professor of church history at the Trinity Evangelical Divinity School, reasoned: "That is, the miracles as such do not prove Jesus to be the Son of God; this power could have been given to Him as a mere man. But indirectly they prove Him to be the Son of God because they prove Him to be a truthful messenger, and this truthful messenger says that He is God. Christ may have wrought miracles and not have been God; but He could not have wrought miracles and said that He was God without being God." [4] He finally concluded: "If it were not so, then we would have the impossible situation of thinking of God as accrediting a liar and sending a messenger with His own divine credentials to lead the world into delusion." [5] It is true that in the future the antichrist will perform miracles and will claim to be God (2 Thess. 2:4, 9), but that is just the point. His will be "lying wonders" because he will be a satanic deceiver. If Christ were not really God, then He too would have manifested the spirit of the antichrist. Some have become confused over Christ's declaration: "The Son can do nothing of himself, but what he seeth the Father do: for what things soever he doeth, these also doeth the Son likewise" (John 5:19 cf. 8:28). Was Christ innately impotent? Did He have only derived power? The great reformed theologian, William Shedd, explained: ". . . he means that he cannot work in isolation or separation from the Father, as if he were another Being." [6] That is why He mentions seeing the Father's works and doing them. The incarnate Christ did not act independently; rather, the divine will and work were one. Both Persons within the Godhead worked together, not separately.

In His postresurrection state, He announced to the disciples on the day of His ascension: "All power is given unto me in heaven and in earth" (Matt. 28:18). This power was both gained through His triumphant death and resurrection and given to Him by the Father. It does not refer to His divine omnipotence. The latter truth was expressed later by Him to John on the island of Patmos: "I am . . . the Almighty" (Rev. 1:8).

The greatest display of Christ's power was in His own resurrection. Paul reasoned that the resurrection declared Christ to be what He claimed to be, the Son of God (Rom. 1:4). Concerning His life, Jesus said: "No man taketh it from me, but I lay it down of myself. I have power to lay it down, and I have power to take it again. This commandment have I received of my Father" (John 10:18). It was impossible for God, eternal spirit and self-existent, to die. It was also impossible for a mere man to raise himself out of a state of death. In fact, Solomon wrote: "There is no man that hath power over the spirit to retain the spirit; neither hath he power in the day of death" (Eccles. 8:8). No man, by an act of his own volition, can release his spirit from his body. If he could, suicide would be much easier to accomplish. Neither can a man by an intense desire prevent his spirit from leaving his body when his time to die has come. In His incarnate state, Christ was given this power. On the cross, He dismissed His spirit or "gave up the ghost" (John 19:30). This power of self-resurrection becomes even more impressive when one realizes that Christ even predicted the very day of His resurrection. Some person, perhaps, could predict the day of his death and the means of that death. This could be true of a criminal on death row, a soldier on the battle front, or a psychotic enamored with suicide. But how could anyone predict the day of his resurrection? At the outset of His ministry, Jesus declared: "Destroy this temple, and in three days I will raise it up" (John 2:19). John explained that "he spake of the temple of his body" (John 2:21). When the antagonistic scribes and Pharisees asked for a sign, Jesus replied: "For as Jonah was three days and three nights in the whale's [fish's] belly; so shall the Son of man be three days and three nights in the heart of the earth" (Matt. 12:40). Privately, to His disciples, He predicted openly His death at Jerusalem and His resurrection on the third day (Matt. 16:21; 17:22–23; 20:17–19; 26:32). Possibly, a person could predict his own resurrection at some indefinite point in the future, but Jesus didn't; He named the day. If He had been raised on the first, second, or fourth day, that would have been a tremendous supernatural event, but that would not have been good enough. It had to be the third day or else Christ would have been a liar, a false prophet. In order to rise on the very day that He predicted, Christ had to have omnipotence to overcome the power of death and of Satan.

Christ also claimed: "That all men should honour the Son, even as they honour the Father. He that honoureth not the Son honoureth not the Father which hath sent him" (John 5:23). He wanted the same faith to be placed in Him as was directed toward the Father (John 14:1). No prophet or apostle appealed for such honor or confidence.

He claimed to be the center of the divine program of salvation.

He chose or elected His own (John 13:18), called them to Himself (John 10:3), sanctified them (John 17:19), sent the Holy Spirit to them (John 16:7, 14), protects them (John 10:28), will raise their bodies (John 5:21), and will judge them (John 5:22). He is the builder, owner, and head of the true church (Matt. 16:18).

He further affirmed that He was sinless. Nowhere did He admit that He needed the salvation of God, although the most sensitive saints of all ages have confessed their moral unworthiness. After he saw a vision of God, Isaiah exclaimed: "Woe is me! for I am undone; because I am a man of unclean lips" (Isa. 6:5). In his defense, Job said to his comforters: "But I have understanding as well as you; I am not inferior to you" (Job 12:3). Later, however, after God revealed Himself to him, Job cried: "I have heard of thee by the hearing of the ear: but now mine eye seeth thee. Wherefore I abhor myself, and repent in dust and ashes" (Job 42:5–6). Paul believed that he could have more confidence in the flesh (religious position and practice) than anyone else (Phil. 3:4), but before God he admitted that he was the "chief of sinners" (1 Tim. 1:15). Such expressions never came out of the lips of Jesus Christ. Even the angelic seraphim cover their faces in the presence of God, showing their moral inferiority to Him (Isa. 6:2). Jesus dared His opponents: "Which of you convinceth me of sin?" (John 8:46). They had secretly watched His every action, had listened to His teaching, and had asked Him trick questions to catch some moral or doctrinal slip, but they never found one on which they could accuse Him. Even the false witnesses could not agree upon their testimony during the trials of Jesus.

Christ did not force people to worship Him, but when some did, He did not rebuke the worshippers. Rather, He gladly received their worship and praised the individuals for doing so. The Magi told Herod the Great that they had come to worship the child who was born King of the Jews (Matt. 2:2). Directed by the star to the right house, there "they saw the young child with Mary his mother, and fell down, and worshipped him: and when they had opened their treasures, they presented unto him gifts; gold, and frankincense, and myrrh" (Matt. 2:11). The worship and the gifts were not directed toward *her* (Mary) nor toward *them* (Mary and Jesus), but toward *him*. The Magi saw nothing blasphemous in their actions, nor did Mary reproach them for their deeds. In His adult life, Jesus openly received worship before multitudes (Matt. 8:2). He accepted it after His resurrection (Matt. 28:17; Luke 24:52). No man or angel should be worshipped. When Satan tempted Christ to fall down and to worship him, Jesus refused: "Get thee hence, Satan, for it is written, Thou shalt worship the Lord thy God, and him only shalt thou serve" (Matt. 4:9-10). Jesus knew who should be worshipped, and yet He willingly received worship. Either He regarded Himself to be the Lord God or else He tempted His fellow men to do exactly what Satan wanted Him to do.

Christ claimed to be the subject of the Old Testament writings. He challenged His opponents: "Search the scriptures; for in them ye think ye have eternal life: and they are they which testify of me" (John 5:39). He later added: "For had ye believed Moses, ye would have believed me: for he wrote of me" (John 5:46). No mere mortal would have made such a presumptuous claim. In His ministry of teaching and healing and in His anticipation of His coming death, He knew that He was fulfilling those relevant Old Testament predictions (Matt. 26:24; Luke 18:31). In His first postresurrection appearance to the group of apostles, He said: "These are the words which I spake unto you, while I was yet with you, that all things must be fulfilled, which were written in the law of Moses, and in the prophets, and in the psalms, concerning me" (Luke 24:44). Christ here referred to the threefold division of the Hebrew Old Testament, consisting of twenty-four books that correspond to the Protestant thirty-nine.

He claimed that salvation could only be found in Him: "I am the bread of life: he that cometh to me shall never hunger; and he that believeth on me shall never thirst" (John 6:35). He stated that no one could go into the Father's presence apart from Him (John 14:6). He declared that the confession or the denial of Him before men determined that person's eternal destiny (Matt. 10:32-33). No patriarch, priest, king, prophet, or apostle mentioned in the Scriptures ever made such exclusive claims. If the author of this book ever said to his students: "I am the way, the truth, and the life; no one comes to the Father but by me," he would be laughed out of the classroom (and rightfully so).

His deity could be seen in His speech, what He said and how

He said it. The multitude was astonished at His sermons "for he taught them as one having authority, and not as the scribes" (Matt. 7:29). The scribes footnoted their talks with references to established rabbinical authorities. That policy has been practiced by men for centuries. Whenever a student wants to reinforce a point in a thesis, he quotes a reputable source that agrees with him. However, Jesus was different. He said: "I say unto you" (Matt. 5:22, 28, 32, 34, 39, 44). He never pointed to any authority higher than Himself. He preached, using the second person imperative ("Do ye") rather than milder forms of command ("Let us do" or "Let them do"). He equated the word and will of the Father with His own word and will (Luke 6:46–49 cf. 11:28). He asserted in His own name as authoritative new commandments: "A new commandment I give unto you, that ye love one another; as I have loved you, that ye also love one another" (John 13:34 cf. Matt. 5:43). His faithful disciples accepted His words as the very words of God.

Since Jesus had a perfect knowledge of the contents of the Old Testament, it is clear that He knew that He was claiming to be Jehovah. No one can successfully charge Him with an accidental trespass into the territory of divine prerogatives. Such claims cannot go unnoticed. In the New Covenant that God made with Israel, He promised: "I will forgive their iniquity, and I will remember their sin no more" (Jer. 31:34). The right to forgive sins belongs only to God, and yet Christ claimed that right. In Capernaum, He said to the palsied man: "Son, thy sins be forgiven thee" (Mark 2:5). The reaction of the scribes was natural: "Why doth this man thus speak blasphemies? Who can forgive sins but God only?" (Mark 2:7). They were both right and wrong in their evaluation of the situation. Their second question was correct, but their first one was erroneous because Christ was no mere man. Christ then defended Himself:

. . . Why reason ye these things in your hearts?
Whether is it easier to say to the sick of the palsy, Thy sins be forgiven thee; or to say, Arise, and take up thy bed, and walk?
But that ye may know that the Son of man hath power on earth to forgive sins, (he saith to the sick of the palsy)
I say unto thee, Arise, and take up thy bed, and go thy way unto thine house.

And immediately he arose, took up the bed, and went forth before them all . . . (Mark 2:8-12).

Speech is cheap; Jesus knew that. It is one thing to say something; it is another to do it. Since the forgiveness of sins involves no outward sense perception, Jesus did what seemed to be more humanly difficult. If He could cause the palsied man to walk by the power of His word, then that same power could remit his sins. Those who remain unconvinced by this logical sequence point to Christ's charge to the apostles after His resurrection: "Peace be unto you: as my Father hath sent me, even so send I you. And when he had said this, he breathed on them, and saith unto them, Receive ye the Holy Ghost: Whose soever sins ye remit, they are remitted unto them; and whose soever sins ye retain, they are retained" (John 20:21–23). These critics claim that just as Jesus delegated authority to forgive sins to the apostles so that same authority was delegated to Him originally by the Father. To them, Christ had an invested, not an innate, authority to forgive. However plausible this argument may appear on the surface, there is one basic flaw. There is no Scripture that states that God delegated such authority to Christ. Christ's actions are very logical when one considers His innate prerogative to remit; however, if He were only claiming delegated authority to forgive the sins of the palsied man, then the reaction of the scribes and His pointed defense seem difficult to explain.

It is the prerogative of deity to raise the dead (1 Sam. 2:6), and yet Jesus said: "For as the Father raiseth up the dead, and quickeneth them; even so the Son quickeneth whom he will" (John 5:21). Akin to that concept is final judgment. Joel said that Jehovah would judge the heathen nations at Armageddon (Joel 3:12). In the Olivet Discourse, Jesus asserted: "When the Son of man shall come in his glory, and all the holy angels with him, then shall he sit upon the throne of his glory: And before him shall be gathered all nations (Matt. 25:31–32).

Christ identified Himself as Jehovah, the Judge of the nations in the last days. He also claimed that He would judge the dead after they had been raised by His voice (John 5:27–29). Speaking about the eternal state (the new heaven and the new earth),

He stated: "Behold, I make all things new" (Rev. 21:5). Just as He had made the first universe, so He would destroy it with a judgment of fire in order to fashion a perfect habitation.

Jesus also claimed these titles ascribed to Jehovah God by the Old Testament: Light (Isa. 69:19–20 cf. John 8:12); I Am (Ex. 3:14 cf. John 8:58); Shepherd (Ps. 23:1; Isa. 40:10–11 cf. John 10:11); and the First and the Last (Isa. 41:4; 44:6 cf. Rev. 1:17; 2:8).

The temple was clearly known as Jehovah's house of prayer (Isa. 56:7) and as His temple (Mal. 3:1). When Jesus drove out the merchants from the temple courtyards, He said to them: "It is written, My house shall be called the house of prayer; but ye have made it a den of thieves" (Matt. 21:13). He used the personal pronoun "my" as a reference to Himself. In defense of the disciples' plucking of grain on the sabbath day, Jesus stated that He was not only the Lord of the sabbath but that He was also greater than the temple (Matt. 12:6, 8). The only one who could be superior to the temple was the one who built the temple and filled the temple with the glory of His presence (cf. Heb. 3:3–4).

One event in Christ's earthly life especially demonstrated that He was God manifest in human flesh. That event was the transfiguration. Many confuse that title with Christ's ascension into heaven (Acts 1), but it is altogether different. One day, Jesus declared to the twelve apostles: "Verily I say unto you, There be some standing here, which shall not taste of death, till they see the Son of man coming in his kingdom" (Matt. 16:28). It is a known fact that all of the apostles have died and that Christ has not yet come to earth to establish His kingdom. What then was the meaning of Christ's statement? Within a week, Jesus took "some" of them (Peter, James, and John) into a mountain. There He "was transfigured before them: and his face did shine as the sun, and his raiment was white as the light" (Matt. 17:2). The English word "metamorphosis" is based upon the Greek word translated "was transfigured" [metemorphothe]. Outwardly, there is a great difference between the form of the moth or butterfly and that of the caterpillar, but they are both forms of the same creature. Paul said that Christ existed in the form (morphe) of God and that He took to Himself the form (morphe) of a servant when he became man. Throughout Jesus' earthly life, the outward expression of His divine nature was covered by a real flesh, bone, and blood body. To men, He appeared to be only a man. Only on this one occasion did Jesus manifest the glory of His deity. At that time, He was metamorphosed. The form of His deity now shone through His human form and covered it. This was a complete reversal of what occurred at His conception in the womb of Mary. Years later Peter under the guidance of the Holy Spirit pointed out that the transfiguration of Christ was a miniature preview of His second advent to the earth (cf. 2 Peter 1:15–18). No man or angel could ever be transfigured because no one possesses a double nature that is necessary for the transformation. Only God who became man could so disclose Himself.

5 The Titles Of Christ

Jesus of Nazareth was identified in several ways by the Biblical authors. The most popular designation was "Christ" and the second was "Lord." The third in frequency was "Son of Man." Of the eighty-four times that it is found in the New Testament, the title "Son of Man" appears only three times outside of the Gospels: by Stephen at his martyrdom (Acts 7:56) and by John during his religious banishment to Patmos (Rev. 1:13; 14:14). It is found in the Old Testament both in the Psalms (Ps. 8:4) and in the prophets (Dan. 7:13). Ezekiel was called "Son of man" throughout his book by God. The title also appears in the apocryphal literature *The Book of Enoch* and *II Esdras* (RSV name) where it refers to the personal messiah. Of all the titles, it was Christ's favorite designation of Himself. At first glance, it might appear that the title stressed only His humanity, but there is also a supernatural quality to the name. He used it with reference to His second advent to describe His coming in His kingdom (Matt. 16:28), in the glory of His Father and the holy angels (Mark 8:38) and in the clouds with great power (Mark 13:26). As the Son of man, He will sit upon the throne of His glory (Matt. 25:31). This application of the title perfectly coincides with Daniel's description of an eschatological figure:

I saw in the night visions, and behold, one like the Son of man came with the clouds of heaven, and came to the Ancient of days, and they brought him near before him.

And there was given him dominion, and glory, and a kingdom, that all people, nations, and languages, should serve him: his dominion is an everlasting dominion, which shall not pass away, and his kingdom that which shall not be destroyed (Dan. 7:13-14).

The Son of man therefore was a Person who shared in the divine glory and sovereignty, who existed before the first century A.D., and who would descend to earth to reign over the nations. By using it, Christ claimed for Himself a distinctive, heavenly, pre-incarnate glory. This explains His subsequent prayer: "And now, O Father, glorify thou me with thine own self with the glory which I had with thee before the world was" (John 17:5). The innate character of the title "Son of man" also carried with it the prerogatives to be surrounded by the angels of God (John 1:51), to either ascend into or descend from heaven (John 3:13), to impart everlasting life (John 6:27), to be ministered unto (Matt. 20:28), to forgive sins (Mark 2:10), to be Lord over both creation and the sabbath (Mark 2:28), and to come into the world to seek and to save that which was lost (Luke 19:10). The title, though, does emphasize His human nature as well. As Son of man, He had no permanent place to lay His head (Matt. 8:20), possessed the capacity to suffer physically, to be betrayed, to be killed, and to be resurrected (Matt. 17:12, 22–23), could minister to others (Matt. 20:28) and could give His life as a spiritual ransom (Matt. 20:28). Although Paul never used the title "Son of man" to describe Christ, yet he understood the double concept of the title:

And so it is written, The first man Adam was made a living soul; the last Adam was made a quickening spirit.

Howbeit that was not first which is spiritual, but that which is natural; and afterward that which is spiritual.

The first man is of the earth, earthy: the second man is the Lord from heaven.

As is the earthy, such are they also that are earthy: and as is the heavenly, such are they also that are heavenly.

And as we have borne the image of the earthy, we shall also bear the image of the heavenly (1 Cor. 15:45-49).

To Paul, Christ was both "the last Adam" (human nature) and "the Lord from heaven" (divine nature). The first human being, Adam, was material before he became spiritual; the body was framed before God breathed into it the life principle or the Spirit. Christ, however, was spiritual (cf. John 4:24) before He assumed a materialistic body.

A second significant title is that of "the Son of God." In the Old Testament, the name was applied to the nation of Israel (Ex.

4:22), to angels (Job 1:6; 2:1; 38:7), and to civil judges (Ps. 82:6–7). The New Testament identified Adam as the son of God (Luke 3:38). When believing sinners are converted, they become children of God by regeneration (John 1:12; Greek text has "children" rather than "sons") and sons of God by spiritual adoption (Gal. 4:5). Thirty-two times it is used as a designation for Jesus Christ. Because of its varied usage, can it be argued that the title inherently implies the possession of deity? The Jehovah's Witnesses will admit that Christ was the Son of God, but they reject vehemently the notion that He was God the Son. Liberals likewise deny that the title involves an eternal, metaphysical sonship. Paul Van Buren, one of the notorious death of God theologians, in his volume *The Secular Meaning of the Gospel,* claimed that the title implied serving obedience and that it described the work of Christ, not His person.[1] Loraine Boettner, however, disagreed. He asserted that the terms "Father" and "Son" "carry with them not our occidental ideas of, on the one hand, source of being and superiority, and on the other, subordination and dependence, but rather the Semitic and oriental ideas of *likeness* or *sameness of nature* and equality of being."[2] It is one thing to say that Jesus Christ *became* the Son of God; it is another to state that He *always was* the Son of the Father. There is no doubt that He accepted the title. Peter named Him: "Thou art the Christ, the Son of the living God" (Matt. 16:16). In His response, He declared: "Blessed art thou, Simon Bar-jona [Son of John]: for flesh and blood hath not revealed it unto thee, but my Father which is in heaven" (Matt. 16:17). At His inquisition before Caiaphas and the religious council, He was asked: "Art thou the Christ, the Son of the Blessed?" (Mark 14:61). Jesus replied: "I am" (Mark 14:62). The high priest apparently quizzed Him a second time: "I adjure thee by the living God, that thou tell us whether thou be the Christ, the Son of God" (Matt. 26:63). This time, Jesus said: "Thou hast said" (Matt. 26:64). This type of answer may seem to be evasive to contemporary speech, but it was the traditional form in which a cultivated Jew replied to a serious question. In other words, the phrase "thou hast said" is the equivalent of "yes." The priests then charged Him with blasphemy, not because of the statements of His accusers, but for His own admission. Moses wrote:

"And he that blasphemeth the name of the Lord, he shall surely be put to death, and all the congregation shall certainly stone him: as well the stranger, as he that is born in the land, when he blasphemeth the name of the Lord, shall be put to death" (Lev. 24:16). If the liberals or the Witnesses are correct, then why did the priests react so violently when Jesus admitted to being the Son of God? Certainly, they knew those Scriptures that applied the title to mere men or angels. To them, Jesus meant something else when He accepted that designation. They knew that He was claiming deity for Himself. In the light of the above passages, it seems strange that Bishop Robinson could boldly write: "It is, indeed, an open question whether Jesus ever claimed to be the Son of God, let alone God." [3] Robinson then cited this verse to show that Christ, by implication, actually denied that He was God: "And Jesus said unto him [rich young ruler], why callest thou me good? there is none good but one, that is, God" (Mark 10:18). His exegesis is most inadequate. Christ was trying to draw out from the ruler a confession that he believed Jesus to be God: "Did you call me 'good' because you believe me to be God?" Jesus didn't say that He was neither God nor good.

A related title is "the only begotten Son." It is used only five times of Christ, all by John (John 1:14, 18; 3:16, 18; 1 John 4:9). The English "only begotten" comes from the Greek *monogenes*, literally meaning "only one [*mono*] of a kind [*genes*]." Elsewhere, it is used of the widow's dead son at Nain (Luke 7:12), Jairus' dying daughter (Luke 8:42), the demon-possessed son of an anonymous father (Luke 9:38), and Abraham's son, Isaac (Heb. 11:17). The latter passage is especially relevant: "By faith Abraham, when he was tried, offered up Isaac: and he that had received the promises offered up his only begotten son. Of whom it was said, That in Isaac shall thy seed be called" (Heb. 11:17–18). Abraham had other physical sons: Ishmael by Hagar (Gen. 16:1–16) before the birth of Isaac and six sons by Keturah after the death of his wife, Sarah (Gen. 25:2). He had only one son by Sarah and both to and through that son, Isaac, the promises of the Abrahamic covenant, the birthright, and the blessing were given. Isaac was unique (one of a kind) because he was the promised heir. How was Christ unique? He was full of grace and truth and manifested the glory of the Father (John 1:14), revealed God to man (John 1:18), was God's expression of love to the world (John 3:16), and became the channel of salvation or condemnation based upon one's belief or rejection of Him (John 3:16, 18; 1 John 4:9). He was God's heir (Rom. 8:17). In the case of the others, all became *monogenes* either through human birth (no other children in the family) or through selection (Isaac instead of Ishmael or Keturah's sons). How did Christ become the only begotten Son? Does this title mean that He became the Son either through divine or human birth or that He was selected out from among others (men or angels)? The answers to these questions center around this messianic declaration: "I will declare the decree: The Lord hath said unto me, Thou art my Son; this day have I begotten thee" (Ps. 2:7 cf. Heb. 1:5; 5:5). Some have concluded that this refers to Christ's baptism. At that event, the Father spoke: "This is my beloved Son, in whom I am well pleased" (Matt. 3:17). However, Jesus acknowledged God to be His Father when He was only twelve (Luke 2:49). He received the Holy Spirit at His baptism because He was the Son. This anointing was linked with His function (to preach and to heal) rather than with His essence (cf. Luke 4:18–21; Acts 10:38).

Many evangelicals have followed the theological direction of the church fathers and have called this begetting the "eternal generation" of the Son. They claim that "this day" is just as eternal as the decree itself. They call it the "universal present" or the "everlasting now." Mikolaski claimed that the generation was from God's essence, not from His creative will or act: "This begetting is an eternal fact of the divine nature; otherwise, if there was a time when the Son was not the Son, then there was a time when the Father was not the Father." [4] If the designation "Father" is an eternal title, then the title "Son" must likewise be so regarded. In his attack upon trinitarianism, Arius, the prototype of the contemporary Jehovah's Witnesses, argued that God was not always the Father and that the Son was not always a son. God became a Father when He brought into being a creature who was named at that time "Son," according to him. The relationship of the three Persons within the divine oneness is an eternal relationship. The choice of "begotten" by the ancient creeds was in preference to "made." The church fathers wanted to point out the unique relationship that existed between the Father and the Son without implying that the Son had a beginning in time. They followed the same procedure with the Holy Spirit when they spoke about the "eternal procession" of the Spirit. They never conceived of a time when the Son was not generated nor when the Spirit did not proceed from the presence of the Father and of the Son.

The most acceptable view is that the eternal decree was fulfilled in the incarnation of the Son of God. John R. Rice referred the term "only begotten" only to Christ's human beginning.[5] When Gabriel answered Mary's question about the means of her conception, he said: "The Holy Ghost shall come upon thee, and the power of the Highest shall overshadow thee: therefore also that holy thing which shall be born of thee shall be called the Son of God" (Luke 1:35). The words "shall be born" and "begotten" come from the same base Greek word. The ministry of the Holy Spirit is always involved in the "begetting" process. The spiritual new birth requires His work (John 3:5; 1 Peter 1:23). All believing sinners have been begotten into the family of God in like manner. There is nothing unique about the new birth of one particular convert as contrasted with innumerable millions who also are saved. And yet, the birth or the begetting of Christ was unique. The Biblical writers chose to use the same Greek root words with purposeful modification. Christ was the *monogenes*, the "only begotten" one. John wrote: "We know that whosoever is born of God sinneth not; but he that is begotten of God keepeth himself . . ." (1 John 5:18). There are three different persons mentioned here: God, "whosoever is born," and "he that is begotten." The phrase "whosoever is born" is the translation of the articular perfect passive participle *gegennemenos* whereas the phrase "he that is begotten" is the translation of the articular aorist passive participle *gennetheis*. The former refers to the believing sinner whereas the latter refers to Christ.

Further proof that the decree (Ps. 2:7) was fulfilled in Christ's incarnation can be seen in Paul's sermon in the synagogue at Antioch in Pisidia: "And we declare unto you glad tidings, how that the promise which was made unto the fathers, God hath fulfilled the same unto us their children, in that He hath raised up Jesus again; as it is also written in the second psalm, Thou art my Son, this day have I begotten thee" (Acts 13:32–33). Since the next verse begins: "And as concerning that he raised him up from the dead . . ." (Acts 13:34, most people conclude that the two "raisings" are necessarily identical. That is why some evangelicals relate the fulfillment of the decree to Christ's resurrection from the dead. However, the "raisings" refer to two different events. The second definitely refers to His bodily resurrection (Acts 13:34–37), but the first refers to His birth. To raise up Jesus in fulfillment of the patriarchal promises was to bring Him into the world to perform His messianic, mediatorial work. Luke used the same concept of "raising" to refer to the birth and accession of the stubborn Pharaoh who oppressed Israel (Acts 7:18) and to the advent of false religious teachers into the church at Ephesus (Acts 20:30). Paul wrote: "For the scripture saith unto Pharaoh, Even for this same purpose have I raised thee up, that I might show my power in thee, and that my name might be declared throughout all the earth" (Rom. 9:17). To raise up seed means to produce children through natural generation (Matt. 22:24). John F. Walvoord, the president of Dallas Theological Seminary, agrees that the second psalm prediction has its fulfillment in the virgin birth of Jesus Christ.[6]

Another important title is that of "firstborn." The Greek word *prototokos* is used nine times in the New Testament. The only non-Christological reference is to the Egyptian firstborn who were killed in the last of the ten plagues (Heb. 11:28). Christ is known as the firstborn of Mary (Matt. 1:25; Luke 2:7), the firstborn among many brethren (Rom. 8:29), the firstborn of every creature (Col. 1:15), the firstborn from the dead (Col. 1:18; Rev. 1:5), the firstborn brought into the world by God and worshipped by angels (Heb. 1:6), and the head of the church (Heb. 12:23). Paul's major Christological section provides the key passage: "Who [Christ] is the image of the invisible God, the firstborn of every creature" (Col. 1:15). The modern Arians, or Jehovah's Witnesses, claim that Christ was the first of a kind, the first and highest of all God's creation, and that He as God's power and in the latter's name created all other things. To them, Christ was the chief of the angels, identified as Michael. Are they correct? Charles Erdman succinctly observed: "The firstborn of all creation might seem to mean that Christ was himself part of the Creation and himself a created Being were it not for the fact that the rest of the paragraph deals wholly with the truth that Christ was not created, but himself was the creator. Paul could not possibly contradict himself so absolutely in one sentence." [7] The basic error that vexed the Colossian church was a form of Judaistic Gnosticism. It taught that matter was innately evil; therefore, God who was pure spirit could never have directly created the material universe Himself. Their cosmogony consisted of a series of successive angelic emanations, each one a little inferior to the one from which it sprang, until finally the last of these aeons created the world. They looked upon Christ as a creature, as one of these emanations, probably the first one. Now, if "firstborn of every creature" meant that Christ was the first creature created, Paul would have been defeating his purpose in writing. This is exactly what the Judaistic Gnostics taught, and to some degree the Witnesses. What would have been the purpose in writing Colossians if he agreed with them in this essential doctrine? Paul was vehemently opposed to the idea that Christ was less than God. Previous sections of this book have demonstrated that fact. The phrase must be seen in its context. It definitely refers to Christ's preexistence and His sovereignty over creation. This fact is proved by the definitive statements introduced by "for" (Col. 1:16–18). The creative powers resided in Him; He was the agency, goal and sustainer of creation. In Near Eastern culture, the firstborn son received the birthright which entitled him to a double inheritance and family leadership upon the death of the father. He was known as the firstborn even if no other children were born into the home. The idea of supremacy soon overshadowed the concept of temporal priority. Later the term was applied to the leading citizens of a community. If Paul wanted to indicate that Christ was the first creature created, he could have used the Greek word *protoktistos* ("first created one"). He did not say "first born of all *other* creation" either. Also, He did not write that Christ *became* the firstborn of all creation. He is the firstborn because of His essence as God and His relationship to the universe as its creator.

Summary

Jesus Christ definitely claimed to be God through His actions and His statements about Himself. The New Testament writers unquestionably believed that Jesus was God manifest in the flesh. They applied Old Testament passages about Jehovah to Him and made their own distinctive claims about Him. A liberal critic, Charles Briggs, admitted: ". . . historically and logically, the divinity of Christ and the Incarnation are bound up with the Virgin Birth, and no man can successfully maintain any one of them without maintaining all." [8] Although this liberal denied all three of those fundamental beliefs, yet he had the common sense to recognize that they were all inseparably involved. Deny one, and you deny the other two; embrace one, and you must consistently accept the others. Bernard Ramm, a recognized evangelical apologist, argued from this thesis: "If God could become incarnate, what kind of man would He be?" [9] He claimed that He would be sinless (absence of any moral blemish), that He would be holy (presence of spirituality), that His words would be the greatest ever spoken, that He would have power over human personality, that He would perform supernatural doings, that He would manifest the love of God, that He would be the most divine man that ever lived, and that His personality would manifest a true humanity. If the Biblical presentation of the person of Jesus Christ is correct, then He must have been God. Once this is accepted, it is only logical to assert that His entrance into the world must have been supernatural. There was only one means that could properly provide the channel for His incarnation: THE VIRGIN BIRTH.

6 Testimony Of Luke

The births of royalty today do not go unnoticed. The advance of media communication has made it possible for the entire earth to know within hours the birth of a new prince or princess. Such was not the case in the first century. When Jesus was born, the record of that event was not published in any newspaper or trumpeted over the air waves. Secular historians paid no attention to it. Only two authentic accounts were produced, and they were not composed until at least fifty years after the actual birth. These narratives form an integral part of the New Testament. Upon them rests the traditional belief of the church in the virgin birth of Jesus Christ.

Testimony of Luke

Luke was a beloved physician (Col. 4:14), a missionary companion of Paul, and an author of two Biblical books (Luke and Acts). Although not a formal apostle, his writings conveyed apostolic authority because of his close association with Paul. Like Timothy (2 Tim. 2:2), he doubtless received his theological instruction from Paul. Since the Book of Acts was probably finished near the end of Paul's first Roman imprisonment (Acts 28: 16–31; A.D. 59–61), it is logical to assume that the Gospel of Luke, the first of the two volumes written to Theophilus (Luke 1:3 cf. Acts 1:1), was written earlier, probably during Paul's two years of imprisonment at Caesarea (Acts 24:27; A.D. 56–58). This would mean that Luke wrote the Gospel after the composition of many of the Pauline volumes, including Galatians and Romans. This fact takes on significance in the light of these key assertions: "the gospel of God . . . concerning his Son Jesus Christ our Lord, which was made of the seed of David according to the flesh" (Rom. 1:1, 3), and "God sending his own Son in the likeness of sinful flesh" (Rom. 8:3), and "But when the fulness of the time was come, God sent forth his Son, made of a woman, made under the law" (Gal. 4:4). Luke, no doubt, had heard Paul teach privately and declare publicly these concepts about Christ's two natures. Perhaps he had even read those verses in the original writings. In any case, Luke brought to his biography of Jesus Christ theological expertise that reflected the beliefs of Paul.

In his opening, dedicatory paragraph, Luke affirmed that he had made a detailed research into the historical data of the life of Christ:

Forasmuch as many have taken in hand to set forth in order a declaration of those things which are most surely believed among us,
Even as they delivered them unto us, which from the beginning were eyewitnesses, and ministers of the word;
It seemed good to me also, having had perfect understanding of all things from the very first, to write unto thee in order, most excellent Theophilus,
That thou mightest know the certainty of those things, wherein thou hast been instructed (Luke 1:1-4).

Previous accounts had only been fragmentary. Luke sifted through them, checking their authenticity against his own private investigation. In Palestine with Paul, he easily could have conducted private interviews with these possible sources: the apostles, John Mark, some of the seventy disciples (cf. Luke 10:1), the women who assisted Jesus' ministry (Luke 8:2–3), early converts (cf. Acts 21:16), the half brothers of Jesus, and possibly even Mary, the mother of Jesus, herself. If Mary had been twenty years old or less at the time of Jesus' birth, she would have only been about seventy-five at the time of the writing of Luke's Gospel. Luke did claim to have had perfect understanding "from the very first" *(anothen)*. Some believe that Luke's knowledge of Christ's life was given by direct, divine revelation since that word is used of the new birth: "born *again*" (John 3:3; or "from above"). However, Luke did use *anothen* later to describe the beginning years of Paul's life (Acts 26:5). It is better to conclude that Luke was referring to the events associated with Christ's birth and infancy. Only Luke deals with the birth announcements about John the Baptist and Jesus, the accounts of their births, the hymns of praise by Elisabeth, Mary, and Zacharias, the circumcision of Jesus, His presentation in the temple when He was forty days old, the worship of Simeon and of Anna, and an event in Jesus' youth. As a doctor, it would have been logical for Luke to have checked out the belief in the virgin birth, a concept that his medical education had regarded to be impossible. Since the record of the virgin birth was included by him, he must have regarded it as one "of those things which are most surely believed among us." This establishes the fact that the virgin birth was a well-developed doctrine by the middle of the first century. In order to gain "certainty" for this unusual event, Luke may have talked to the elderly Mary. A subtle hint for this conclusion may be gleaned from this expression: "But Mary kept all these things, and pondered them in her heart" (Luke 2:19, 33, 51). What Mary kept as a private matter, she willingly disclosed to a physician (a common trait of most women). Since Luke assured Theophilus that he had checked everything thoroughly, then if he was wrong on the origin of Jesus (the very first event recorded), why should Theophilus or anyone else believe him about Christ's adult years? As a physician, then, the factuality of the virgin birth would set the tone for the entire book.

Here, then, is his record:

And in the sixth month the angel Gabriel was sent from God unto a city of Galilee, named Nazareth,

To a virgin espoused to a man whose name was Joseph, of the house of David; and the virgin's name was Mary.

And the angel came in unto her, and said, Hail, thou that art highly favoured, the Lord is with thee: blessed art thou among women.

And when she saw him, she was troubled at his saying, and cast in her mind what manner of salutation this should be.

And the angel said unto her, Fear not, Mary: for thou hast found favour with God.

And behold, thou shalt conceive in thy womb and bring forth a son, and shalt call his name JESUS.

He shall be great, and shall be called the Son of the Highest: and the Lord God shall give unto him the throne of his father David:

And he shall reign over the house of Jacob for ever, and of his kingdom there shall be no end.

Then said Mary unto the angel, How shall this be, seeing I know not a man?

And the angel answered and said unto her, The Holy Ghost shall come upon thee, and the power of the Highest shall overshadow thee: therefore also that holy thing which shall be born of thee shall be called the Son of God.

And, behold, thy cousin Elisabeth, she hath also conceived a son in her old age: and this is the sixth month with her who was called barren.

For with God nothing shall be impossible.

And Mary said, Behold the handmaid of the Lord; be it unto me according to thy word. And the angel departed from her (Luke 1:26-38).

Several important observations should be made about this narrative. First, it is permeated with a supernatural tone: the presence and the speech of an angel, the activity of God, and the overshadowing ministry of the Holy Spirit. This is *not* a normal birth announcement. As Wilbur Smith reasoned: "The supernaturalism of Christianity rests distinctly and solidly upon the supernaturalism of its founder, Jesus Christ." [1] From the manger to the cross, the word "extraordinary" marks the life of Jesus. The above supernatural factors were not interpolated, but were an innate part of what actually happened. If the supernatural concepts were removed, then the narrative would be so destroyed as to have no meaning or logical sequence. Second, Mary was identified. She definitely was a virgin at the time of this encounter. The word is mentioned twice (1:27) and her reply to the angelic prediction supports that conclusion: "How shall this be, seeing I know not a man?" (1:34). The Revised Standard Version has done a great disservice to the Greek text with this translation: "How can this be, since I have no husband?" She *had* a legal husband, Joseph, although they were still in the betrothal period. A young Jewish couple could either be betrothed by their respective parents or betroth themselves. This legal binding contract could only be broken by the judges who established it. The betrothal involved a twelve-month waiting period, designed mainly for the protection of the husband's inheritance. If the woman was pregnant at the time of betrothal, her immorality would then be discovered. Thus, the husband could be released from his contract without any shadow of adultery hanging over him. Mary had never had any intimate sexual relationships with any man, including Joseph, either before or during their betrothal period. Whereas the angel went to Zacharias and announced to him the birth of his forthcoming son, John, the angel came to Mary, the mother to announce the birth of Jesus. Although an angel later did appear to Joseph, it was only after the conception had occurred and after he had discovered Mary's pregnancy (Matt. 1:18–25). This further substantiates the fact that Joseph was not the paternal father of Jesus. Mary's future child was designated in various ways: Jesus, great, Son of the Highest, Son of David, king, holy thing, and Son of God. Never was he called by the angel "the son of Joseph." Her child would be *called*, not that He would *become*, the Son of God. Christ was not holy simply because He was virgin born; rather, He was virgin born because He was holy in His eternal Person and because He had been set apart for this messianic task. He said that He had been sanctified before He was sent into the world (John 10:36). From the production of the egg out of Mary's ovary to the actual birth, the fetal state in Mary's womb was entirely under the controlling, sanctifying ministry of the Holy Spirit. Under such superintendence, there was protection both against a miscarriage and natural birth defects.

Luke gave other indications in these first two chapters that Jesus was virgin born. When Mary visited Elisabeth, the latter, filled with the Holy Spirit, exclaimed to her: "Blessed art thou among women, and blessed is the fruit of thy womb. And whence is this to me, that the mother of my Lord should come to me?" (Luke 1:42–45). She identified Mary's fetal child as "my Lord," a messianic title that implied deity (cf. Luke 2:11; Ps. 110:1). She pronounced a blessing both upon Mary and Jesus, but noticeably omitted any reference to Joseph or to any other man. She concluded her Spirit-inspired praise: "And blessed is she that believed: for there shall be a performance of those things which were told her from the Lord" (1:45). This referred to Mary's total submission to the divine will contained in Gabriel's announcement: "Behold the handmaid of the Lord; be it unto me according to thy word" (1:38). The comparison of these two verses to the content of the angel's prediction definitely reveals a knowledge of a conception by God without human, male fertilization.

In Mary's magnificat (1:46–55), she made no reference to Joseph. God received the entire credit for her conception. She stated among other things: "For he that is mighty hath done to me great things; and holy is his name" (1:49). This could possibly refer to the predicted overshadowing power of God at the time of conception (cf. 1:35).

In his narrative of the birth of Jesus, Luke reported that Joseph went to Bethlehem "to be taxed with Mary his espoused wife, being great with child" (2:5). If Mary had been pregnant by Joseph, Luke no longer would have identified her as "his *espoused* wife" (cf. 1:27). The period of betrothal would have ended with the first act of sexual intercourse between them. Even after Joseph took unto him (into his house) Mary after the explanation of the angel, he "knew her not till she had brought forth her firstborn son" (Matt. 1:24–25). There were no sexual intimacies between Joseph and Mary before their betrothal, after the betrothal but before her conception, and after her conception but before the birth of Jesus. The first sexual relationship between them occurred after the birth of Jesus.

The fact that Luke referred to Joseph and Mary as "his parents" (2:27, 41) should not be construed as either a confession or a contradiction. Mary was both Jesus' legal and natural mother; as the betrothed husband of Mary, Joseph became the legal father of Jesus when he named Jesus at His circumcision. The Jewish community thought that Joseph was also the natural father of Jesus: "And they said, Is not this Joseph's son?" (Luke 4:22). Luke always balanced his usage of "parents" with other expressions to bring the reader back to the realization of Christ's uniqueness. The phrase "Joseph and his mother" (2:33, 43) provides such an example. If Jesus had been the natural son of both of them, why didn't Luke continue to refer to them as "his parents" or as "his father and his mother"? Simeon addressed himself to Mary, not to Joseph, when he spoke about the coming death of Jesus (2:34).

When Jesus was twelve, he was accidentally left behind in

Jerusalem when Joseph and Mary started out on their return trip to Nazareth. They later found Him in the temple, carrying on a dialogue with the religious elders. Mary then spoke to Him: "Son, why hast thou thus dealt with us? behold, thy father and I have sought thee sorrowing" (2:48). In public, Mary had to refer to Jesus as Joseph's son in order not to arouse any suspicion about His origin. The virgin birth would have been impossible to explain at that time, and the only other alternative would be for people to suspect an illegitimate birth. She had to express the relationship between Joseph and Jesus in that fashion. Jesus, however, reacted: "How is it that ye sought me? wist ye not that I must be about my Father's business?" (2:49). The contrast is between "thy father" and "my Father." The temple was not Joseph's business, but rather the domain of God the Father. This first recorded remark from the lips of Jesus definitely shows that in His consciousness He was aware that He was the Son of God even though He was only twelve years old in His human development.

In a past generation, John A. Scott, professor of Greek at Northwestern University for forty years, in his volume *We Would Know Jesus*, wrote: "Luke was not only a Doctor, and a historian, but he was one of the world's greatest men of letters. He wrote the clearest and the best Greek written in that century. . . . Without Luke, we never could have had a report from a competent man of science on the birth from a Virgin. If Jesus had two human parents, why did the shrewd Gentile Physician never suspect that fact?" [2] That question still stands today. After making a thorough investigation into the human beginnings of Jesus, Luke was certain that He was virgin born, and he wanted Theophilus and us to be likewise convinced.

7 Testimony Of Matthew

Whereas Luke recorded the announcement of the birth of Jesus to Mary before the conception, Matthew's narrative contained an explanation to Joseph after the conception:

Now the birth of Jesus Christ was on this wise: When as his mother Mary was espoused to Joseph, before they came together, she was found with child of the Holy Ghost.

Then Joseph her husband, being a just man, and not willing to make her a public example, was minded to put her away privily.

But while he thought on these things, behold, the angel of the Lord appeared unto him in a dream, saying, Joseph, thou son of David, fear not to take unto thee Mary thy wife: for that which is conceived in her is of the Holy Ghost.

And she shall bring forth a son, and thou shalt call his name JESUS: for he shall save his people from their sins.

Now all this was done, that it might be fulfilled which was spoken of the Lord by the prophet, saying,

Behold, a virgin shall be with child, and shall bring forth a son, and thy shall call his name, Emmanuel, which being interpreted is, God with us.

Then Joseph being raised from sleep did as the angel of the Lord had bidden him, and took unto him his wife:

And knew her not till she had brought forth her firstborn son: and he called his name JESUS (Matt. 1:18-25).

This passage, first of all, reveals that Joseph and Mary were legally married or betrothed (1:18). She was called "his wife" twice (1:20, 24). He was called "her husband" (1:19). In order to dissolve the union, he had planned to divorce her (1:19; meaning of "to put away"). Secondly, although legally married, there had been no sexual relationships between Mary and Joseph. Joseph discovered Mary's pregnant condition "before they came together" (1:18). After he did take Mary into his house, an act signifying to the public that the legal union was now about to be consummated in a physical act, they continued sexual abstinence until after the birth of Jesus (1:25).

Third, Joseph knew that the child Mary was carrying was not his own. He discovered her pregnancy; she did not reveal the fact to him. In most loving homes, the wife is more than happy to disclose to her husband the fact of her pregnancy. There is no strong indication that the community knew about Mary's condition. Joseph was not the last to know; he was the first and the only one to know (with the exception of Elisabeth and possibly Zacharias). This view is also supported by his action to divorce her. Joseph was in a dilemma. As a just man, he could not continue the legal betrothal into a lasting marriage because of Mary's presumed infidelity and because of his obedience to the Mosaic law: "When a man hath taken a wife, and married her, and it come to pass that she find no favour in his eyes, because he hath found some uncleanness in her: then let him write her a bill of divorcement, and give it in her hand, and send her out of his house" (Deut. 24:1). On the other side, he did love her, and because he did, he did not want to shame her publicly. He chose a private divorce procedure over a harsh, public exposure. Remember what the Pharisees did with the woman taken in adultery. They brought her to the temple before the multitudes and Jesus and said to Him: "Master, this woman was taken in adultery, in the very act. Now Moses in the law commanded us, that such should be stoned, but what sayest thou?" (John 8:4–5). It is true that the involved parties in the sin of adultery could be sentenced to death (cf. Lev. 20:10; Deut. 22:22), but strict conformity to that legislation was not widely practiced in the first century. Joseph opted for the relaxed method. The phrase "while he thought" is not an adequate translation of the aorist passive participle *enthumethentos*. Literally, it means "after he thought." After debating what to do, he made up his mind, and then retired to bed.

A fourth observation is that Mary's pregnancy was ascribed to the power of the Holy Spirit. Mary was in a humanly impossible situation. Although she knew that she had been faithful to Joseph, yet she also knew that she had submitted to the will of God to be the human mother of the divine-human messiah. How could she adequately explain what had happened? Could she tell Joseph that an angel had visited her, that he told her that she would have a child by the power of the Highest, and that it had actually come to pass? Humans are known for their attempts to justify their wrongs, but this explanation would have been totally unbelievable. This is why it was necessary for God to defend the moral integrity of Mary through the angelic messenger: "Joseph, thou son of David, fear not to take unto thee Mary thy wife: for that which is conceived in her is of the Holy Ghost" (1:20). Matthew himself confirmed this statement of origin (cf. 1:18). The command not to fear had double importance. Joseph had feared to take an adulteress as his wife, but now that fear had been removed; Mary had no illicit affair with another man. But now, would Joseph dare to touch sexually one who had been overshadowed by God? Would he view her as so pure and delicate as not to be tarnished by his sexual passion? He had to be told that a normal marital union, including sexual intercourse, could be experienced by him.

Fifth, Joseph was instructed to take Mary into his house and to name the child (1:20–21). The act of naming the child publicly declared that he would be claiming the legal paternity of the child. This he did (1:25). The community, thus, believed Joseph to be the real father as well as the legal parent. There was suspicion when Elisabeth wanted her son to be named "John" rather than "Zacharias" (cf. Luke 1:57–63). They perhaps thought that the priest was sterile and that Elisabeth had had an illicit affair with a man bearing the name "John." Note that the angel did not use the typical birth announcement to men: "She shall bear a son *to thee*." It was so spoken to Abraham (Gen. 17:19) and to Zacharias (Luke 1:13). Both Abraham and Zacharias were sexually involved in the respective conceptions of Sarah and Elisabeth, but Joseph had nothing to do humanly with Mary's pregnancy.

A slight exegetical problem is found in this passage: Did the angel speak the words of 1:21–22 to Joseph or do these two verses reveal Matthew's editorial comment upon the angelic explanation? In other words, did the angel quote the Old Testament text of Isaiah 7:14 to convince Joseph that his explanation was scriptural? It is plausible that this is what occurred. If so, Matthew gave his apostolic approval by his incorporation of the quotation into his narrative. However, it is probably better to regard the two verses as Matthew's own interpretation. In other places, he used the prophetic formula to show the fulfillment of the Old Testament in the life and ministry of Christ: the birth site of Bethlehem (2:5–6), His presence in Egypt (2:15), the decree to slay the male infants in and around Bethlehem (2:17), the dwelling at Nazareth (2:23), the character of the ministry of John the Baptist (3:3), the ministry in Galilee (4:14–16), the healing ministry (8:17), the tenderness of Christ (12:17–21), the unbelief of Israel (13:14–15), His parabolic teaching (13:35), and the purchase of the potter's field with Judas' money (27:8). Pike and Kennedy argued that Matthew was arbitrary in his attempts to put the events of Christ's life into a "fulfilled prophecy motif." They wrote: "If Matthew had had a Hebrew Bible to work with, he wouldn't have had to fulfil the prophecy of 'a virgin birth.' And so it goes item after item. It is not mythological. It is seeing to it that prophecies are fulfilled." [1] The Hebrew text has the word *almah* translated as "virgin" here. These liberal critics referred to the fact that the Greek translation of the Hebrew Old Testament, the Septuagint version, used the Greek *parthenos* for the Hebrew *almah*. Pike and Kennedy viewed this as an unfortunate word exchange. They also contended that Matthew used the Greek *parthenos* rather than the Hebrew *almah* as the basis for his equation of the birth of Jesus by Mary without a human father to the prophecy of Isaiah. However, both *parthenos* and *almah* refer to sexual virginity and regardless of which Old Testament text he used, that concept was there. These critics, by their criticism of Matthew, also revealed their denial of any supernatural ministry of the Holy Spirit in the lives and compositions of the Biblical authors. They see the sixty-six books as mere human literary works.

The child was to bear the name "Jesus," not "Emmanuel." In the past, the latter term signified the providential presence of the God of Israel (Isa. 8:8 cf. 43:2; Jer. 1:8), but here it is applied to His personal presence in Jesus. The *New Scofield Reference*

Bible observed: "Why was Jesus not actually called 'Immanuel'? According to the Hebrew usage, the name does not represent a title but a characterization, as in Isaiah 1:26 and 9:6. The name 'Immanuel' shows that He really was 'God with us.' Thus the deity of Christ is stressed at the very beginning of Matthew." [2]

In the light of the above observations, it is difficult to ascertain why the well-known commentator, William Barclay, a professor at the University of Glasgow and a member of the Church of Scotland, would call the virgin birth a "crude fact." He added: "The Virgin Birth is a doctrine which presents us with many difficulties; and it is a doctrine which our Church does not compel us to accept in the literal and the physical sense. This is one of the doctrines on which the Church says that we have full liberty to come to our own belief and our own conclusion." [3] The doctrine of the Virgin Birth only presents difficulties to those who question the literal, historical accuracy of the Gospel narratives, the sovereignty of the Almighty, and the deity of Jesus Christ. Strangely, Barclay asserted that the emphasis is on the Spirit of God in Matthew's version: "The essence of Matthew's story is that in the birth of Jesus the Spirit of God was operative as never before in this world." [4] Certainly the activity of the Spirit was essential to the conception by Mary, but the central figure of the narrative and of the entire book of Matthew was Jesus Christ (1:1 cf. 1:18).

In his first two chapters, there are other indications that Matthew firmly believed in the virgin birth of Jesus Christ. In the genealogical list, he used the literary format: A begat B, and B begat C, etc. (1:2−15). However, when he came to the relationship of Joseph to Jesus, he changed the style radically: "And Jacob begat Joseph the husband of Mary, of whom was born Jesus, who is called Christ" (1:16). The word "whom" is the genitive feminine singular relative pronoun *hes*. Its grammatical antecedent could only be the female Mary, not the masculine Joseph. All forms of the word "begat" were aorist active indicatives until Matthew switched to the aorist passive indicative for the birth of Jesus by Mary. These abrupt changes definitely show that Joseph did not beget Jesus, but that he was simply the husband of Mary. The Greek manuscript evidence for the textual reading adopted by the Authorized Version (King James, 1611) was and is extremely strong. It seems strange that the editors of *The Greek New Testament* (Kurt Aland, Matthew Black, Bruce Metzger, and Allen Wikgren), published by the United Bible Societies, should indicate that there is some degree of doubt to this reading which they had adopted into their text. Moffat, in his *New Translation of the New Testament*, utilized this variant reading: ". . . and Joseph (to whom the virgin Mary was betrothed), the father of Jesus, who is called 'Christ'." A footnote to the *New English Bible* reads: "One early witness has: Joseph, to whom Mary, a virgin, was betrothed, was the father of Jesus . . . ." In the original 1946 edition of the Revised Standard Version, there was no footnote comment on this verse, but when the entire RSV Bible was printed in 1952, it carried this footnote: "Other ancient authorities read: Joseph, to whom was betrothed the virgin Mary, was the father of Jesus who is called Christ." These minor readings are only supported by the Ferrar group of minuscules, the Sinaitic Syriac Version, and the Von Soden text. Why did these men opt for a weak textual variation in favor of the strongly authenticated reading? Lenski, a noted Lutheran exegete of a past generation, wrote: "Here we meet a typical example of critical methods. Of all the ancient texts in existence, including all the ancient versions, one (usually identified by the symbol Ss) is singled out as containing a reading which the critics use to rid themselves of the virgin birth. All Greek texts and all other versions are set aside, for this one Syriac translation, the codex Ss and its reading, is made *the original reading*, and all other texts are regarded as an accommodation to the doctrine of the Virgin Birth." [5] These textual editors have not been honest with the evidence. They have permitted their anti-supernaturalism to overcome their intellectual objectivity. There is no reason why any evangelical should do what Louis Matthews Sweet did in his article on the virgin birth in the conservative *International Standard Bible Encyclopedia* (ISBE). He accepted the reading that Joseph begat Jesus, claimed that Matthew simply copied the existing genealogical records, and argued that "begat" should be interpreted in a legal, not a physical, sense.[6] If the passage is simply taken in its normal meaning, then Matthew was affirming that Joseph had no physical, paternal relationship to Jesus.

When the magi, or wise men, came to Jerusalem, they asked Herod: "Where is he that is born King of the Jews? for we have seen his star in the east, and are come to worship him" (Matt. 2:2). Worship of royalty was practiced in the Near Eastern world, but the worship of an infant to the exclusion of his parents was not known. To the Jew, the worship of any human being was both repulsive and blasphemous. These magi, who had calculated from ancient Jewish prophecy the exact time that the messiah would appear (Dan. 2:31–45; 7:1–28; 9:24–27), saw something distinctive in this child. Later, "when they were come into the house, they saw the young child with Mary his mother, and fell down, and worshipped him; and when they had opened their treasures, they presented unto him gifts; gold, and frankincense, and myrrh" (Matt. 2:11). The magi did not worship Mary, or Mary and Joseph, or Mary, Joseph and Jesus; they worshipped *only* Him. Their gifts were presented only to Him also.

Throughout this chapter, Matthew identified Mary as "his mother" (2:11, 13, 14, 20, 21). Joseph is never designated as the father of Jesus. To warn Joseph about Herod's hostility, the angel said to the former: "Arise, and take the young child and his mother, and flee into Egypt" (2:13). Why didn't the angel simply charge: "Take *your* child and *your* wife"? Later the angel used the same command and changed only the destination: "Arise, and take the young child and his mother, and go into the land of Israel" (2:20). In obedience to both angelic commands, Matthew recorded that Joseph took the child and *his mother* (2:14, 21). According to Matthew, the sojourn in Egypt fulfilled the prophetic statement: "Out of Egypt have I called my son" (2:15 cf. Hosea 11:1). Jesus was God's son, not Joseph's. The testimony of Matthew is crystal clear as to the virgin origin of Jesus Christ.

8 Testimony of The Church Fathers

The doctrinal faith of the evangelical does not rest upon what the ancient bishops and presbyters believed, but rather upon the authoritative statements of the Word of God. And yet, what the church fathers believed *is* important to the contemporary theological scene. Those clerics were close to the first century. If they did not believe in the virgin birth of Jesus Christ, then can we point to this doctrine as a traditional, foundational truth? There should be some continuity between the belief of the church in the apostolic age and that of the second century.

Adolf Harnack, a German rationalistic theologian who denied the deity of Jesus Christ, nevertheless admitted: "It is certain that already in the middle of the second century, and probably soon after its beginning, the birth of Jesus from the Holy Ghost and the Virgin Mary formed an established part of the Church tradition." [1] Ignatius of Antioch in Syria (c. 110) defended the virgin birth in his volumes: *To the Ephesians; To the Smyrnaeans; To the Magnesians;* and *To the Trallians*. Since he argued against the Docetic heretics, he had to prove not just the virgin birth, but also a real, ordinary human birth. The Docetics denied that Christ had a real human body; to them, He only appeared to have one. They perceived Christ's ministry as a theophanic manifestation, not a real incarnation. Aristides (c. 125) defended the doctrine in his *Apology for the Christians to the Roman Emperor*. Justin Martyr (c. 150) wrote two such defenses: *Apology* and *Dialogue with Trypho*. Unfortunately, he tried to justify the Christian doctrine with analogies drawn from pagan accounts of unusual births. Tatian contributed his *Diatessaron* and *Address to the Greeks*. Melito of Sardis referred to his belief in the virgin birth in three volumes: *Discourse on the Cross; Discourse on the Soul and Body;*

and *From Melito the Bishop, On Faith*. Irenaeus (c. 175) wrote *Against Heresies*. Clement of Alexandria used *The Instructor* and *Miscellanies* in his defense. Hippolytus composed: *Refutation of All Heresies; Treatise on Christ and Anti-Christ; On Proverbs XXIV;* and *Against Beron and Helix*. Tertullian referred to the doctrine in: *On the Flesh of Christ; The Prescription Against Heretics; Against Praxeas;* and *Against Marcion*. Origen, in the first half of the 'third century, defended the virgin birth in his famous volume *Against Celsus*.

The second century saw the production of the *Gospel of the Ebionites*, a book that did not contain the first two chapters of Matthew. The Ebionites saw Jesus only as a natural-born son. In the *Gospel of Luke used by Marcion*, the narrative began at the third chapter. These two volumes show that these two heretical groups believed that the opening chapters both of Matthew and Luke taught the virgin birth of Christ. They did not seek out a natural or a symbolic explanation for those accounts; rather, they simply cut them out of their "scriptures." In the closing years of the southern kingdom of Judah, Jeremiah had his scribe Baruch write down what the former dictated. Later, when Jehudi read that scroll before king Jehoiakim, "he cut it with the penknife, and cast it into the fire that was on the hearth, until all the roll was consumed in the fire that was on the hearth" (Jer. 36:23). They did not like what they had read and heard, therefore they destroyed the scroll. They burned the paper, but they did not consume the truth. Jeremiah recorded their reaction to their deed; "Yet they were not afraid, nor rent their garments, neither the king, nor any of his servants that heard all these words" (Jer. 36:24). The Ebionites and the Marcionites did the same thing in their generation. Today, the liberal establishment has not physically removed the contents of those chapters from the modern versions of the Bible, but they have mentally stripped them of any literal, historical meaning.

The Apostle's Creed, produced in Gaul about the fifth or sixth century, was based upon an old Roman baptismal confession, dated as early as A.D. 200. Both Tertullian and Irenaeus used the latter in the middle of the second century. The key text read: "Born of the Holy Ghost and the Virgin Mary." The convert, before his baptism, had to include that truth in his confession of faith. That shows that the doctrine of the virgin birth was so firmly entrenched in the life of the early church that it was deemed to be one of the fundamental doctrines. No one would be admitted into a Christian assembly nor recognized as a genuine believer without faith in it.

Thomas Boslooper, an ordained minister in the Reformed Church in America, in his recent volume *The Virgin Birth*, concluded: "The literature that has been preserved for us from the ante-Nicene, Nicene, and post-Nicene fathers shows that the church fathers from Ignatius through Thomas Aquinas treated the theme of the virgin birth as a gem which was placed in many different settings: the explanation of the origin of the redeemer, the answer to the question of how the Logos entered the world, an aid in describing the relationship between the two natures of Christ, and the basis for Marianism." [2] Although evangelicals would reject some of the false concepts built upon the doctrine of the virgin birth (e.g., elevation of Mary), they nevertheless would argue that "the baby should not be thrown out with the bath water." The fact of the virgin birth stands regardless of the many attacks made by its enemies or the faulty distortions and extensions manufactured by its friends.

9 Erroneous Concepts

   The incarnation, the virgin birth, and the deity of Jesus Christ form an inseparable triad. They must all either be accepted or denied to maintain logical and Scriptural consistency. One concept cannot be embraced to the denial of the other two, or vice versa. According to the Koran, the bible of the Moslem religion, Jesus was virgin born, but He was not God incarnate. This position fails to grapple with the implications of such a birth: Did Jesus possess a real humanity without a human father? Did he have a sin nature? Why was He worshipped? To accept only one of the three basic tenets is to assume an intellectual stance that cannot be defended.

   Other false concepts have also developed. First of all, the incarnation does not involve a dual parenthood for Jesus. Contemporary liberals often talk about the incarnation while they are at the same time denying a literal virgin birth. In most cases, they believe that Jesus was the natural-born son of Joseph and Mary. A. T. Robertson, the great Southern Baptist Greek scholar, penned: "Incarnation is far more than the Indwelling of God by the Holy Spirit in the human heart. To admit real incarnation and also full human birth, both father and mother, creates a greater difficulty than to admit the Virgin Birth of Jesus begotten by the Holy Spirit, as Matthew here says, and born of the Virgin Mary." [1] Incarnation, by definition, means that the eternal God has become flesh. There is no way that natural generation could provide the acceptable channel. It could never be said that the mere son of Joseph and Mary was really "God." This would be an attempt to deify humanity, to make man into God.

   Secondly, the incarnation does not involve transubstantiation. The latter is supposed to occur when one material substance is literally changed into another. The medieval alchemists tried unsuccessfully to change lead into gold. According to the Roman Catholic Church, transubstantiation occurs at the sacrament of the mass when the priest blesses the elements of the wine and the wafer. To them, a miracle happens whenever and wherever this clerical function is repeated: The wine literally becomes the blood of Christ and the wafer or bread literally becomes His flesh. To the participant, the wine and the wafer may still physically taste and feel as though they have not changed, but actually they have. Faith should supersede the senses. At the moment of blessing and reception, the wafer and the wine cease being those. Their molecular structures have been radically altered. Evangelicals have strongly resisted this dogmatic declaration of the Roman Catholic Church, and they shou'd equally resist any form of transubstantiation that might be attached to the incarnation. When the Bible believer affirms that God became man, he does not mean that deity was turned into humanity. When God became man, He did not cease being God. How could God ever be less than what He is? At the incarnation, God acquired a human nature. Before the virgin conception, God the Son only had the divine nature; after that event, He had both the divine nature and a human nature. The Jehovah's Witnesses actually embrace the concept of transubstantiation when they teach that Michael, an angelic creature, became Jesus, a human being, at the virgin conception. According to them, Jesus was no longer an angelic or spirit being during His lifetime on the earth. To them, the process of transubstantiation was reversed at His "resurrection" when the humanity of Jesus was changed into a spirit being once again. The end result is a denial of the *bodily* resurrection. The incarnation actually produced an eternal union of the two natures in the person of Christ. After His death and resurrection, He continued to be both divine and human. He did not surrender His humanity at His death any more than He gave up His deity at the virgin conception. A genuine incarnation and transubstantiation are two diametrically opposed concepts.

Third, the incarnation should not be viewed as a mere theophany, an appearance or manifestation of God. It should not be construed as a human episode in the divine life. Theophanies did occur in the pre-Christian era. God appeared *as* man to Abraham (Gen. 18:1–33), Jacob (Gen. 32:24–30), Moses (Ex. 24:9–11; 34:5–6), Joshua (Josh. 5:13–15), the parents of Samson (Judg. 13:2–22), Isaiah (Isa. 6:1–5), and Shadrach, Meshech, and Abednego (Dan. 3:24–25). These were appearances, not incarnations. God assumed the likeness of man to communicate with man. It is true that mention is made of God's back parts, hands, eyes, feet, and other terms descriptive of human members, but these should be regarded as "anthropomorphisms." This is a literary device used by God and by the Biblical writers to describe God's activities. It is the ascription of human characteristics to the being of God for the purpose of intelligent communication. Since God is spiritual, a spirit being, how could He reveal to man that He *sees* everything when He Himself does not have a literal physical eye complete with lens, retina, and optic nerve? Such anthropomorphisms were necessary literary accommodations to reduce the nature of the infinite divine being down to the perceptive level of the finite human understanding. When the various theophanies occurred in the Old Testament age, there were no virgin births associated with them. God merely assumed an adult likeness of man. A real incarnation and virgin birth involve nine months of fetal life, a natural childbirth, and normal human development.

Fourth, the incarnation and the virgin birth do not cause Mary to become "the mother of God." Elisabeth called her "the mother of my Lord" (Luke 1:43), but nowhere in Scripture was Mary ever called the mother of God. A human mother exists before her offspring. To be the mother of God, one must of necessity exist before God. This, of course, is impossible. God is eternal; He had no beginning. It is true that Jesus Christ was both God and man, but He was God long before Mary's conception. Mary rightfully mothered the humanity of Jesus, but not His deity. It is true that God was within her womb, but she did not cause that to happen. Mary did not produce the person of Jesus Christ; rather, she produced the human nature that God the Son took to Himself in His incarnation. Unfortunately, not only has the Roman Catholic Church adopted this erroneous terminology, but critics can also point to its usage by these respected church fathers:

Origen, Athanasius, Eusebius, and Cyril of Jerusalem. These men did not believe Mary to be God or divine just because they called her "the mother of God." In their defense of the deity of Christ, they unwittingly chose this designation for her. Often defenders of the truth can use improper language that can later be misconstrued by those who don't understand the original meaning. The Roman Catholic dogma is not based upon accurate Biblical exegesis, but rather upon this philosophical syllogism: Mary is the mother of Jesus; Jesus is God; therefore, Mary is the mother of God. Such a sequence fails to consider seriously the union of the two natures in the single person of Jesus Christ and His preincarnate deity.

Fifth, a similar error would make the Holy Spirit to be the father of Jesus' human nature. Thus, Jesus would become the Son of the Spirit. Neither God the Father nor God the Spirit took the place of a human father in the production of Christ's humanity. Just as Mary did not mother the deity of Christ, neither did the Spirit father His humanity. Jesus became the human son of Mary, but He always was the son of God the Father.

Sixth, the incarnation and the virgin birth do not involve the immaculate conception of Mary. The Roman Catholic Church declared as a dogma in 1854 that Mary herself was conceived apart from sin. This means that no sin nature was transmitted by Mary's parents to her, that she lived a sinless life, free from sinful deeds and thoughts, and that she mothered Jesus apart from any sin. To maintain the sinlessness of the human nature of Christ, many Catholic theologians have justified this position. To them, how could a sinful woman produce a sinless son? Their solution to the moral and theological dilemma took them back one generation: Mary was conceived apart from sin. But this doesn't solve any problems; it creates new ones, more complex than the first. In the conception of Jesus, there was only one parent involved, whereas in the conception of Mary, there were two. There was no act of physical intercourse in the conception of Jesus, but there was a sexual union of Mary's parents. A new question must then be asked: How could two sinful people produce a sinless daughter? To attribute the sinlessness of Christ to the sinlessness of Mary is both unscriptural and theologically illogical. Her conception and birth were not unique. She was shapen in iniquity and in sin her mother conceived her (cf. Ps. 51:5). Like all descendants of Adam and Eve, she was a sinner both in nature and in deed (Rom. 3:23; 5:12). Only by the over-shadowing, sanctifying ministry of the Holy Spirit was she prevented from passing on to her fetus her sinful character.

Mary, herself, acknowledged her human sinfulness in her magnificat, the song of praise given in reaction to Elisabeth's eulogy: "And my spirit hath rejoiced in God my Saviour" (Luke 1:47). If Mary had been sinless, holy, and the mother of God, why did she need a Saviour? Only sinners need to be saved. She saw her position before God as "the low estate of his handmaiden" (Luke 1:48). She did admit that all future generations would call her "blessed" (Luke 1:48), but that Greek word for "blessed" is *makarios*, the same word used to identify all believers in the Beatitudes (Matt. 5:3–11). There was nothing uniquely or innately *makarios* about the person of Mary. When Jesus was forty days old, this event transpired:

And when the days of her purification according to the law of Moses were accomplished, they brought him to Jerusalem, to present him to the Lord;
(As it is written in the law of the Lord, Every male that openeth the womb shall be called holy to the Lord;)
And to offer a sacrifice according to that which is said in the law of the Lord, a pair of turtledoves, or two young pigeons (Luke 2:22–24).

The full law for the ceremonial purification of the mother after the birth of a son is now listed:

Speak unto the children of Israel, saying, If a woman have conceived seed, and born a man child: then she shall be unclean seven days; according to the days of the separation for her infirmity shall she be unclean.
And in the eighth day the flesh of his foreskin shall be circumcised.
And she shall then continue in the blood of her purifying three and thirty days; she shall touch no hallowed thing, nor come into the sanctuary, until the days of her purifying be fulfilled. . . .

And when the days of her purifying are fulfilled, for a son, or for a daughter, she shall bring a lamb of the first year for a burnt offering, and a young pigeon, or a turtledove, for a sin offering, unto the door of the tabernacle of the congregation, unto the priest:

Who shall offer it before the Lord, and make an atonement for her; and she shall be cleansed from the issue of her blood. This is the law for her that hath borne a male or a female.

And if she be not able to bring a lamb, then she shall bring two turtles, or two young pigeons; the one for the burnt offering, and the other for a sin offering: and the priest shall make an atonement for her, and she shall be clean (Lev. 12:2–4, 6–8).

The total dedication of the firstborn male to God occurred at the forty-day interval; Joseph and Mary did this for the infant Jesus. At the same time, Mary offered a sacrifice of two birds as a burnt offering and as a sin offering for her own uncleanness and atonement. Now, there was nothing morally sinful about the action of begetting the sinless Christ. As a sinner, however, she became ceremonially impure through the birth procedure. If Mary had been sinless and had remained so during the pregnancy and postpregnancy periods, there would have been no need for her to have offered any type of sacrifice whatsoever. Jesus never offered any sacrifice for Himself because He was never morally or ceremonially impure. This could not be said of Mary.

Others confessed that Mary was not innately holy nor that she had become such through her conception of Jesus. The angel Gabriel announced to her: "Hail, thou that art highly favoured, the Lord is with thee: blessed art thou among women" (Luke 1:28). The five words "thou that art highly favoured" are the translation of one Greek word *kecharitomene*. Grammatically, it is a perfect passive participle and means "one who has been endued with grace by another." Mary had become a recipient of grace, not its source. Grace is the impartation of divine favor apart from human merit. The virgin Mary was no more morally virtuous than any other virgin descendant of David. God chose her to be the channel of the redeemer because He wanted to, not because she was the most spiritual young woman available. This does not mean that her moral integrity was simply incidental. Certainly God could not have used a prostitute, nor would He have wanted to do so. The second angelic phrase, "Blessed art thou among women" is the translation of *eulogemene su en gunaixin*. The word "Blessed" (*eulogemene*) is also a perfect passive participle, meaning "one who has been well spoken of or blessed by another." Mary was not the source of blessing or the Blessor, but rather its recipient. Also, she was blessed *among* women, not *above* women. Later the angel added: "for thou hast found favour [or grace] with God" (Luke 1:30). She found the favor or grace outside of herself, not within her person.

Elisabeth, by the Holy Spirit, said to Mary: "Blessed art thou among women, and blessed is the fruit of thy womb" (Luke 1:42). The Greek word for "Blessed" in both cases is a perfect passive participle. The blessing resided in God's choice of Mary and her womb to channel His Son into the human race. Thus the egg produced by her ovary was blessed; the human fetus that grew in her womb was blessed; and she was blessed as the channel of God's purpose. This word for "blessed"—*eulogemene*—must be contrasted with *eulogetos*, used both by the inspired Zacharias (Luke 1:68) and the apostle Paul (Eph. 1:3) to refer to God the Father. Only God is blessed in Himself; because He is, He is able to bless others, including Mary. Elisabeth did not subsequently contradict herself when she identified Mary as "the mother of my Lord" (Luke 1:43). In this context, the phrase refers to the human mother of Israel's messianic king, not to the originator of deity.

Finally, the incarnation and the virgin birth do not involve the perpetual virginity of Mary. In a way, this concept is tied up with the view that Mary remained sinless throughout her life. To some, sexual relationships, even within the marital union, bear some sinful taint in the satisfaction of physical desires. To the angelic announcement, Mary asked: "How shall this be, seeing I know not a man?" (Luke 1:34). A Catholic writer, Aloys Dirksen, made this comment: "Since Mary was married at the time and expected shortly to take up life with St. Joseph, her disturbance and her question indicate that, with her husband's consent, she had made a vow to remain a virgin. Catholic tradition has always taught this." [2] This explanation manifests a theological bias. Mary's reaction only confirmed her virginity up to the time of the angelic visit. She had never known a man intimately nor was she presently involved with Joseph. There is no indication that

she planned never to have sexual intercourse with her own betrothed husband. It is true that Joseph "knew her not till she had
brought forth her firstborn son" (Matt. 1:25), but he did know
her sexually after the birth of Jesus. Note the time word "till"
(heos).

Some have argued that the usage of "firstborn" automatically
implies that Mary must have had at least one other child; however, since the title involves family inheritance and lordship, the
only child in a family could also be called "firstborn." There are
other indications in Scripture that Mary and Joseph had children
of their own after the birth of Jesus. Since this is so, Mary's virginity ended with the first sexual act between Joseph and her. In
Jesus' hometown of Nazareth, the citizens were astonished at His
teaching: "Whence hath this man this wisdom, and these mighty
works? Is not this the carpenter's son? is not his mother called
Mary? and his brethren, James, and Joses, and Simon, and Judas? And his sisters, are they not all with us?" (Matt. 13:54–56
cf. Mark 6:2–3). Some have argued that the brothers and the
sisters refer to Joseph's children by a previous marriage or to family cousins. However, the words *adelphoi* and *adelphai* normally
refer to typical brother-sister relationships. Elisabeth was a
cousin of Mary, but that word for "cousin" was *suggenis*. The
people at Nazareth wondered why Jesus was so different from the
rest of that paternal-maternal family. Some have tried to equate
Jesus' brethren with His disciples. Jesus did emphasize a spiritual
relationship within the family of God that superseded mere physical ties (Matt. 12:46–50), but in so doing, He did not say
that human bonds did not exist (cf. Luke 14:26). After He turned
water into wine, "he went down to Capernaum, he, and his
mother, and his brethren, and his disciples: and they continued
there not many days" (John 2:12). That passage shows a distinction between the two groups: the brethren and the disciples. During Jesus' earthly ministry, His brothers rejected His
messiahship (John 7:3–5, 10). Since they were not at Golgotha,
Jesus delivered the physical care of Mary into the hands of the
apostle John (John 19:26–27). His brothers did not become believers until Jesus appeared to them after His resurrection (John
20:17 cf. 1 Cor. 15:7). Then they associated themselves with

their mother, the apostles, and other Christians in the upper room, awaiting the advent of the Holy Spirit (Acts 1:12–14). Paul even identified James as "the Lord's brother" (Gal. 1:19), one of the three spiritual pillars of the Jerusalem church (Gal. 2:9). There is no justifiable reason to maintain the perpetual virginity of Mary or even of Joseph, as Thomas Aquinas, the founding father of philosophical Roman Catholic theology, argued.

10 Physical Implications

      The beginning of human life within the womb of a woman is still a mystery in spite of all the scientific research to understand it. The union of the male sperm with the female egg, the structure and the mitosis of a living cell, and the genetic complexities all defy total human comprehension and reproduction. Transferred to the arena of the incarnation, the mystery becomes even more hidden. Paul was absolutely correct when he affirmed: "And without controversy great is the mystery of godliness: God was manifest in the flesh . . ." (1 Tim. 3:16). How does human life begin? Yes, but more than that, how did human life begin in the womb of Mary apart from human male fertilization? Can any life form develop from an egg cell without fertilization to produce a living creature? Scientists call the latter possibility "parthenogenesis," which literally means "virgin born."

    In his excellent volume *To Be As God*, an investigation into the attempts of science to create and to control life, Bolton Davidheiser, a biologist with a doctorate from Johns Hopkins University, pointed out examples of parthenogenesis that naturally occurred among lower life forms and that were artificially produced through laboratory experimentation.[1] The eggs of rotifers develop parthenogenetically with the result that males are very rare in some species, and rather unknown in others. Within the world of the honey bees, the unfertilized eggs develop into drone or males. Tichomiroff in 1886 was the first scientist to attempt artificial parthenogenesis. His experiments with the development of the unfertilized eggs of silkworms proved to be successful. Morgan and Mead (1896–1900) started the eggs of sea urchins and marine worms to develop by placing them in various salt solutions or concentrated sea water. In 1900, Loeb obtained normal larvae of sea urchins by treating the unfertilized eggs chemically. More recently, shad have been produced in significant commercial amounts through the activation of eggs by an electric current. Some frogs have been gained by activating unfertilized eggs through a puncture with a fine needle. Pincus (1939–1940) produced several rabbits, all female, through chemical and temperature effects upon the ova.

Although parthenogenesis has never occurred within the human race, some evangelicals have defended the virgin birth of Christ by pointing to its counterparts among the lower life forms. The recognized apologist Wilbur Smith wrote: "No critic of the Virgin Birth today would dare speak of the "biological impossibility" of such an event. We dismiss this particular criticism without further discussion." [2] However, it is theologically and scientifically dangerous to attempt to justify the occurrence of divine miracles through allusion to naturalistic phenomena. Even if it could be demonstrated that parthenogenesis could be artificially induced among women, it would only prove that Jesus was human. It could not prove the reality of the incarnation. In fact, it would become an argument against the incarnation and the uniqueness of Christ's birth. The Bible believer should not defend the possibility of virgin births within the human race; rather, he should argue that virgin births *cannot* happen naturally or artificially and that the only reason why Christ was virgin born was because of the miraculous ministry of the Holy Spirit. Miracles, by nature, are nonrepeatable. Ramm rightly concluded: "The virgin birth of Jesus Christ is a biological miracle. Being a miracle it is not capable of biological proof, analogies of parthenogenesis in the biological world being irrelevant. Its justification must be documentary, historical, and theological. We can offer no biological proof of the virgin birth, and yet we can offer justification of this biological miracle." [3] Actually, parthenogenesis among mammals does not provide a supportive analogy for the virgin birth of Jesus. Geneticists have demonstrated that mammals have two X chromosomes in the females and that the males have both an X and a Y chromosome. Thus, when an unfertilized egg cell would duplicate its chromosomes in response to some artificial stimulation, the resultant being would have to be female. This was true of the Pincus rabbits. Therefore, according to natural law, the virgin conception of Mary should have produced a daughter, not a son. Since the human male determines the sex of the offspring, it is obvious that the sex of the human nature of Jesus was determined by the "sex" of His divine nature. He was God the Son, not "God the Daughter." His entrance into the unfertilized egg of Mary caused the latter to develop without the expected duplication of the female X chromosomes. Within the world of birds, butterflies, moths, and some fish, the genetic structure is just the opposite. The males have the similar pair of chromosomes whereas the females have the odd. The parthenogenetically produced life forms would always then be males.

Although it would appear that Mary did not determine the sex of her fetus, yet it should not be concluded that she did not contribute anything to Christ's human nature. It was *her* egg that God the Son entered. However, one view claims that Mary did not even contribute the egg. This view would maintain that Christ's human nature was created by God and merely placed into Mary's sustaining womb.[4] Just as God created the human nature of Adam, so God made the human nature of Jesus. Although this view would solve the problem of Christ's sinless human nature, it eliminates His genetic relationship to the human race which was necessary for redemptive purposes. Christ's direct relationship both to Israel and to the human race would only be legal, not physical. Thus, He could only be the legal son of Mary, the legal son of David, the legal son of Abraham, and the legal son of Adam. However, this view violates clear exegesis of key passages. How could Jesus be the seed of the woman (Gen. 3:15) when the woman did not furnish the egg? How could it be said that a virgin conceived (Matt. 1:23 cf. Luke 1:31)? According to this position, all Mary needed to do was to bring forth the son. There is a difference between conception and birth, and yet it was predicted that Mary would do both. Paul said that Christ "was made of the seed of David according to the flesh" (Rom. 1:3 cf. 2 Tim. 2:8).

The genetic relationship of Jesus to Mary, to Israel, and to the human race is absolutely necessary for the proper interpretation of Matthew's analysis of Jesus' sojourn in Egypt: "When he [Joseph] arose, he took the young child and his mother by night, and departed into Egypt: and was there until the death of Herod: that it might be fulfilled which was spoken of the Lord by the prophet, saying, Out of Egypt have I called my son" (Matt. 2:14–15). Critics have charged Matthew with a false application of Hosea's historical allusion: "When Israel was a child, then I loved him, and called my son out of Egypt" (Hosea 11:1). Hosea did refer to the exodus of Israel out from Egyptian bondage under the leadership of Moses. How then could Matthew apply this passage to Jesus? The only suitable explanation is that Jesus was genetically present in His physical ancestors who walked out of Egypt fifteen hundred years before. This is one concept that defies a rationalistic approach to the Scriptures, but nevertheless, it is true. This is not the only place where such a genetic reference was used. To prove the superiority of the priesthood of Christ according to the order of Melchisedec over that of the Levitical order, the author of the book of Hebrews selected a historical event out of the life of Abraham. After Abraham had defeated the kings who had kidnapped Lot, he encountered on his return trip home Melchisedec, the king of Salem and the priest of God (Gen. 14:17–24). Abraham paid tithes to him, and Melchisedec blessed the patriarch in return. The book of Hebrews then argued: "And as I may so say, Levi also, who receiveth tithes, payed tithes in Abraham. For he was yet in the loins of his father, when Melchisedec met him" (Heb. 7:9–10). In physical descent, Levi was actually the great grandson of Abraham: Abraham, Isaac, Jacob, then Levi. Abraham was childless at the time of his encounter with Melchisedec, but yet, all of his future children were genetically present in him. There could have been no Levi if there had not been any Jacob; there could have been no Jacob if there had not been any Isaac, and there could have been no Isaac, if there had not been any Abraham. So it was with Jesus. He was genetically present in His physical ancestors in Egypt; when they came out, He came out. He not only came out genetically in the historical past, but He also came out of Egypt in His own lifetime. Now, if there had been no real genetic, physical relationship to Mary, then Matthew would have been wrong in applying Hosea's reference to Jesus. Mary was the real mother of the human nature of Jesus, not just the channel through whom the divinely created humanity could be carried in the womb and be born.

There is no indication that God fertilized the egg of Mary through the work of either the Father or the Spirit. Rather, she conceived without human or divine fertilization when God the Son not only entered her womb, but also the egg in her womb, under the superintending ministry of the Holy Spirit.

11 Jesus Was Truly Human

How could the immutable God change and become man? How could one person be both divine and human at the same time? If Jesus was truly human, doesn't that mean that He also possessed a sin nature? How else could He be tempted? The reality of the virgin birth of Jesus Christ automatically raises questions such as these.

A True Humanity

In His eternal essence, God is basically a spirit being, not physical (John 4:24), and yet He created man in His own image (Gen. 1:27). Thus, the image of God in man is not mere physical likeness (cf. Deut. 4:15–16; Isa. 40:18–25; Rom. 1:23; 1 Tim. 1:17; 6:16). Man, like God, is basically a spirit being. The seat of his personality, involving intellect, emotion, and will, resides within his spiritual part, not his material body. After God breathed into the physical frame, Adam became a living human being. Today, when death occurs, the spirit is separated from the body. For the Christian, the immaterial self goes to be with Christ in heaven while the body goes into the ground. In contrast with the animal and the vegetable kingdoms, man is a moral personality with an innate sense of oughtness, a conscience to distinguish right from wrong. When the sperm of Adam fertilized the egg of Eve, a new life was conceived in their human image (Gen. 5:1, 3). Through procreation, man has passed his image, which he received from God, from generation to generation. Unlike God though, man must have a material body in and through which his spiritual self can function. A child then receives his body and spirit (his material and spiritual properties) at the moment of conception.

The question is now obvious: Did God the Son receive at the

moment of incarnation and virgin conception a real human body and a real human spirit? If He received one but not the other, could He possess a true humanity?

The testimony of Scripture is clear: Jesus was a true man. John wrote that "the Word [Christ] was made flesh" (John 1:14). The verb "was made" is the translation of the deponent aorist middle indicative *egeneto*. Literally, the word *came to be* flesh. He was not human, but in a completed event in His past (conception), He became totally human. The concept of "flesh" involves more than inanimate skin and bone; it describes all that man is. In order for flesh to have will, desires, or emotions (cf. John 1:13), it must have personality. In his first epistle, John wrote: "Hereby know ye the Spirit of God: Every spirit that confesseth that Jesus Christ is come in the flesh is of God: and every spirit that confesseth not that Jesus Christ is come in the flesh is not of God: and this is that spirit of antichrist" (1 John 4:2–3). The issue of Jesus' true humanity was and is so important that true orthodoxy is dependent upon it.

Paul said: ". . . God sending his own Son in the likeness of sinful flesh, and for sin, condemned sin in the flesh" (Rom. 8:3). The likeness refers to the "sinful" flesh; Christ was in the flesh, but He did not have the sin nature with its evil deeds and thoughts that all other men possessed. This passage also shows that "flesh" refers to more than just the material body; otherwise, Paul would have been teaching the Gnostic error that physical things in themselves are innately evil. Later Paul also stated: "God was manifest in the flesh" (1 Tim. 3:16).

The book of Hebrews speaks clearly to this subject. The author wrote: "Forasmuch then as the children are partakers of flesh and blood, he also himself likewise took part of the same; that through death he might destroy him that had the power of death, that is, the devil" (Heb. 2:14). Whatever flesh and blood means, the children (mankind) had it, and so did Jesus. Later he added: "For verily he took not on him the nature of angels; but he took on him the seed of Abraham" (Heb. 2:16). Christ did not become an angel at His incarnation; He became a man. In fact, He became a Jewish man, racially speaking. The author constantly referred to the sufferings of Christ, climaxed by His death (Heb. 2:9–10, 14,

18; 5:7–9; 10:12; 12:2). Genuine human sufferings include more
than physical pain, but also emotional and mental anguish. If the
sufferings of Christ were not more than physical, then an animal
spiked to a wooden cross or a tree cut with a sharp axe would
elicit the same type of pain.

In what ways was Christ's true humanity specifically manifested? First, He had a normal human birth (Matt. 2:1; Luke
2:11). The miracle of the incarnation occurred at the conception,
not at the birth. Apart from the overshadowing ministry of the
Holy Spirit, Mary's pregnancy was no different than that of any
other human mother. Her giving of birth was accompanied with
the normal birth pains. If spanked, the child Jesus cried as His
lungs filled with fresh air. There was nothing magical or extraordinary about the birth procedure of Jesus. For this reason, contemporary evangelicals commend the early church for its rejection
of these apocryphal gospels that reported fanciful legends about
the infancy and childhood of Jesus: *The History of the Blessed
Virgin Mary; The Gospel of the Nativity of Mary; The Gospel of
the Infancy; The Gospel of Pseudo-Matthew;* and *The Gospel of
Thomas.* One reported that a midwife was cured of palsy when she
touched the infant Jesus. Another stated that Mary gave the Magi
a band of swaddling cloth in exchange for their gifts. Later they
threw the cloth into a fire, but it did not burn. The *Arabic Gospel
of the Infancy* contains an account of the infant Jesus speaking:
". . . when He was lying in His cradle said to Mary His mother:
I am Jesus, the Son of God, the Logos, whom thou hast brought
forth, as the angel Gabriel announced to thee; and my Father has
sent me for the salvation of the world." [1] Later the Gospel
claimed that Jesus struck His boyhood friends dead for slight
offences. Such accounts are repulsive and completely foreign both
to the integrity of Christ's character and the testimony of Scripture.
Jesus never performed any miracles until after His baptism and
His anointing by the Holy Spirit. John actually stated that the first
miracle done by Jesus was the turning of water into wine at Cana
in Galilee (John 2:11). Although Jesus Christ was God, His humanity was a true and perfect humanity. He was not like Superman, a visitor to earth from the fictional planet Krypton. His eyes
did not have X-ray vision, and bullets would not have bounced off

His chest. He was not a science-fiction character with Martian, Frankenstein, or Dr. Jekyll-Mr. Hyde qualities. He was truly human as we are. There was no difference between us. We are neither more nor less human than He was. When His hands, feet, and side were pierced, blood came out of the wounds. It would have been the same for us.

Jesus underwent normal human development. From infancy to age twelve, He "grew, and waxed strong in spirit, filled with wisdom: and the grace of God was upon him" (Luke 2:40). From age twelve to adulthood at thirty, He "increased in wisdom and stature, and in favour with God and man" (Luke 2:52). He developed as any child, boy, or young man would have grown up, with two major exceptions: He had no sinful tendency, and He always did the will of God. His development reflected the original purpose of God for man. In His human growth, He became what all men could have achieved were it not for the presence and transmission of the sin nature. Man, today, is in a fallen state; Christ was not. Jesus experienced normal, human intellectual, physical, spiritual, and social growth. In a sense, He was more a man than we are. His life was the normal human life; ours is not. It is as if we are trying to run a one-hundred-yard dash with an hundred-pound weight attached to our backs. That is not normal! In His life experiences, Christ had no weight of sin to keep Him from fulfilling all goals outlined for man by God. Thus, Jesus had to learn how to walk, to talk, to feed Himself, and to work with His hands. His knowledge and application of Old Testament texts to real situations stemmed not from his divine omniscience, but from His keen intellect and His desire to learn.

Jesus had normal physical experiences. Not only was He born, but He died. The physical sufferings of His death by crucifixion were no different from those two thieves or from thousands who had felt the sting of Roman capital punishment. He hungered both after fasting (Matt. 4:2) and after sleeping (Matt. 21:18), thirsted after a journey (John 4:7) and during physical pain (John 19:28), became fatigued after a long walk (John 4:6), and slept for the restoration of His body (Matt. 8:24; Mark 4:38).

He also had normal emotional experiences. He was tempted to

sin (Matt. 4:1–11), became angered at the harsh prejudice of the
Pharisees (Mark 3:5) and at the pride of His disciples (Mark
10:14), was moved with compassion over the spiritual needs of
the multitudes (Matt. 9:36) and over the physical needs of the
infirmed (Mark 1:41), wept at the tomb of Lazarus (John
11:35), and loved both non-Christians (Mark 10:21) and believers (John 13:1). Jesus was definitely "a man of sorrows, and
acquainted with grief" (Isa. 53:3). His soul experienced both joy
(John 14:11) and anxiety (Matt. 26:37; John 12:27).

He had normal spiritual experiences. He fasted (Matt. 4:2),
perfectly obeyed the written Word of God (Matt. 4:4, 7, 10), and
prayed (Matt. 14:23). He was sensitive to His relationship to
God, always in total communion with His Father and completely
yielded to the enabling ministry of the Holy Spirit.

Whereas animals have a body and a life principle, the center of
their functions, every human being has a body (*soma*), a soul
(*psuche*), and a spirit (*pneuma*). Theologians have debated between dichotomy and trichotomy. Does man have three separate
parts (1 Thess. 5:23) or does he have two parts, material and
spiritual? Are spirit and soul simply two designations of the same
entity, or are they two different functions of man's spiritual nature?
Regardless of the answers, Christ possessed all that every man
has. He had a true body, complete with every physical organ:
heart, brain, lungs, kidneys, etc. He had a human spirit. In the
upper room, "he was troubled in spirit, and testified, and said,
Verily, verily, I say unto you, that one of you shall betray me"
(John 13:21). He had a human soul. In the garden of Gethsem-
ane, He said to His disciples: "My soul is exceeding sorrowful,
even unto death: tarry ye here, and watch with me" (Matt.
26:38). The ancient error of Apollinarianism taught that the
divine Logos took the place of the human soul in the person of
Jesus. Its advocates later altered its position and stated that the
Logos united with a body and an irrational animal soul. But in
either case, it denied to Jesus a true and a complete humanity.
When God the Son became flesh, He became all that man is. If He
is denied a body, a soul, or a spirit, then to that extent, He was
only partially human. Christ was not one half man nor one third
man, but total man.

At the incarnation, Christ became eternally wedded to a human nature. He did not throw off His humanity or any part of it at His death, resurrection, or ascension. The mortal, corruptible body in which He died did change into an immortal, incorruptible body, but it was still a human, material body. A *man* rose from the dead, appeared to His disciples, ascended into heaven, is today at the right hand of the Father, and will return to the earth in some future day. When Saul of Tarsus saw the resurrected Christ on the road to Damascus, he said: "Who art thou, Lord?" (Acts 9:5). In His reply, the Savior used His human name: "I am Jesus whom thou persecutest" (Acts 9:5). Today there is one mediator between God and man; it is "the *man* Christ Jesus" (1 Tim. 2:5).

Contrasted with Adam, Christ's humanity had a different expression. Adam was created and began an adult existence the very first day he lived. The human nature of Jesus was conceived within a mother's womb like any other human being, but apart from human fertilization. Jesus experienced a fetal state, a real birth, and normal development, but Adam did not. Christ had a navel; Adam had none. Thus, mankind in a sense is more like the humanity of Jesus than the humanity of Adam. Both Adam and Jesus were equally human, but they gained their humanity in different ways.

12 Two Natures
One Person

God the Son gained a true humanity through the virgin conception, but how could two different natures exist within the same person? Would not one nature be dominated by the other? Would not each nature have to surrender some of its qualities in order for each to coexist beside each other? Could Jesus Christ be truly God and truly man at the same time? The liberal Bishop Robinson did not think so. He wrote: "The supranaturalist view of the Incarnation can never really rid itself of the idea of the prince who appears in the guise of a beggar. However genuinely destitute the beggar may be, he *is* a prince; and that in the end is what matters." [1] English literature, however, affected the theology of Robinson more than the Pauline epistles: "For ye know the grace of our Lord Jesus Christ, that, though he was rich, yet for your sakes he became poor, that ye through his poverty might be rich" (2 Cor. 8:9). Although the prince assumed the role of the pauper, he never was reborn as a pauper and never joined the beggarly nature to his own royal nature. In the fictional story, the prince and the pauper were two separate persons; in the Scriptures, the divine nature and the human nature were united into one person. That is the difference between human imagination and divine revelation.

However, the hypostatic union of the two natures in Christ remains as a supreme paradox. Berkhof, the great Reformed theologian, rightly wrote: "The doctrine of the two natures in one person transcends human reason. It is the expression of a supersensible reality, and of an incomprehensible mystery, which has no analogy in the life of man as we know it, and finds no support in human reason, and therefore can only be accepted by faith on the authority of the Word of God." [2] How then can the staunch believer in the deity of Christ correlate and communicate the Scriptural data about His person to other Christians, let alone to the critical, unbelieving world? Because of semantic problems, what words should be chosen as vehicles of these sacred concepts? F. F. Bruce commented that in the early church "Greek and Latin terms had to be used in new and specialized senses to fit a set of data with which these languages had not been called upon to deal before. And one thinker might use a term in a completely adequate sense while another would use it in a sense which did much less than justice to the data of biblical revelation and Christian experience." [3] Today, that ancient problem still exists. Unfortunately, at times two evangelicals can even give varying theological slants to the same term or can use two different words to describe the same entity. However, traditional evangelical orthodoxy has generally agreed to the usage of the words "nature" and "person" in the description of the complex union of the divine and the human within Christ. The concept of *nature* refers to "the sum-total of all the essential qualities of a thing, that which makes it what it is." [4] The term *person* means "a complete substance endowed with reason, and consequently, a responsible subject of its own actions." [5] When the two concepts are brought together, then "a person is a nature with something added, namely, independent subsistence, individuality." [6] Thus, God is a person with a divine nature. An angel is a person with an angelic nature. A man is a person with a human nature. However, an animal has an animal nature, but it is not a person. Persons are marked by personality, consisting of the qualities of self-consciousness and self-determination. The evangelical position therefore states that Christ was one of the three persons within the divine oneness and that after His incarnation, He was still one person but with two natures, divine and human.

Whereas evangelicals approach the subject of the incarnation from the starting point that Jesus Christ was the eternal Son of God, liberals begin with the presupposition that Jesus was merely a man. From that basis, they go on to explain what they mean by the usage of the creedal terms: incarnation, virgin birth, and hypostatic union. Ever since the advent of the Age of Reason, they claim that it is unworthy of man to accept on the authority of Scripture what is clearly contrary to their way of thinking.[7] Therefore, they believe that they must interpret the theological expressions of Scripture which support the deity and the humanity of Christ in such a way as to make them compatible with the modern scientific mentality. Thus, to Schleiermacher, Jesus was a man with a supreme God consciousness. Ritschl saw in Jesus a man having the value of a God. Wendt viewed Him as a man standing in a continual inward communion of love with God. Jesus was a God-filled man, according to Beyschlag, and Sanday saw Him as a man with an inrush of the divine in the subconsciousness. The desire of the liberal to give verbal assent to creedal terms with a denial of their orthodox meaning has often led to ridiculous, ambiguous statements. Here is Bishop Robinson's concept of the hypostatic union: "The life of God, the ultimate Word of Love in which all things cohere, is bodied forth completely unconditionally and without reserve in the life of a man—the man for others and the man for God. He is a perfect man and perfect God—not as a mixture of oil and water, of natural and supernatural—but as the embodiment through obedience of 'the beyond in our midst', of the transcendance of love." [8] Robinson contended that the orthodox, creedal language with its literal meaning would not be bought by the modern man in the market place of ideas and life experiences. Does he really believe that the union employee who works the eight to five shift will more readily accept the concept that Jesus Christ is "the embodiment of the transcendance of love" rather than the fact that He is both God and man? For twenty centuries, both learned and simple men have accepted the latter description with no mental reservations even though they did not have total comprehension of Christ's mysterious person. Other liberals are very severe in their criticism of both the terms and their respective meanings of orthodoxy. Hugh Schonfield, the Jewish author of the stormy bestseller, *The Passover Plot*, made this assessment:

What underlies their testimony is the original Jewish-Christian doctrine which has been termed adoptionist, because in keeping with the Scriptures it held that Jesus on that occasion had been received into sonship of God. This teaching became overlaid in Gentile Christianity by the concept of the Incarnation, which asserted in pagan fashion that Jesus had been born Son of God by a Spiritual act of fatherhood on God's part which fertilised the womb of the Virgin Mary, and then went on to claim by an elaboration and partial misunderstanding of Pauline theology that the Son of God had eternally pre-existed and was manifested on earth in Jesus, who thus from birth was God dwelling in a human body by a hypostatic union of the two natures.[9]

Schonfield claimed that the doctrine of the union of the two natures in Christ was the end result of an evolutionary theological sequence. Christ's divine sonship went backwards from the baptism to the birth to eternity. The first step was Jewish, the second pagan, and the third Pauline. It claims that a man became deified by zealous, easily influenced followers. Such a charge may seem impressive, but there is no factual support, historical or Biblical, for it.

To the Biblical authors, Jesus Christ was both God and man. In the same sentence, they referred to His two natures. Paul penned: "and of whom as concerning the flesh Christ came, who is over all, God blessed forever" (Rom. 9:5). Earlier he wrote: "Concerning his Son Jesus Christ our Lord, which was made of the seed of David according to the flesh; and declared to be the Son of God with power, according to the spirit of holiness, by the resurrection from the dead" (Rom. 1:3–4). To them, there was no contradiction that Jesus was both fleshly human and spiritually divine.

In the contemporary expression of the hypostatic union, Bible-believing Christians should be careful to use exact language. Since God breathed out the very words of Scripture (Matt. 5:18; 2 Tim. 3:16), we should not add to or subtract from those concepts. First of all, Christ must be seen as a theanthropic person ("the" $=$ divine; "anthropic" $=$ human). He did not have a theanthropic nature which would have been the result of a merger between the divine and the human natures. There are different natures (divine, angelic, human, animal) but there is no such entity as a theanthropic nature. He is a *theanthropic* person, not an anthropotheistic person. There is a definite reason why the divine precedes the human in that compound adjective. He was divine *before* He became human. He was God manifest in flesh. It could be said that

He was humanized deity but never that He was deified humanity. He was the God-man, but not the man-God. He was neither a divine man nor a human god.

Secondly, Jesus Christ had two natures, but not two persons. He was not schizophrenic. At His incarnation, He did not take into union with Himself another person with a human nature. He did not become two persons with two natures. At that time, His divine person partook of a human nature; His divine nature did not assume a human nature. At the virgin conception, He did not acquire a personality for He already was a person. Rather, He gained a new nature; otherwise, He would have been impersonal in His eternal divine existence. It is incorrect to say that the person of Christ was only divine though. He is both human and divine, and yet, He was a divine person before the incarnation occurred. Was the human nature that He acquired impersonal? Most say that it was because of a fear in equating "personal" with "personality." Berkhof, however, said that Christ "assumed that nature into personal subsistence with Himself. The human nature has its personal existence in the person of the Logos. It is inpersonal rather than impersonal." [10] In no way was Christ a dual personality. Within the divine essence or nature were the three Persons: Father, Son, and Holy Spirit. The Son could address the Father, and the Father could reply to the Son. But there is no indication that the divine nature ever carried on a verbal communication with the human nature within the single person of Christ. Nor did Jesus ever use "we" or "us" in reference to His theanthropic person. He always used "I" or "me" because He was just one Person. When God created, He said "Let us" because there are three persons within the divine oneness. There is no direct analogy between the trinitarian oneness of God and the theanthropic person of Christ. In the former, there are three persons but only one nature, divine; in the latter there is only one person with two natures, human and divine.

Third, Jesus Christ was one person with two different kinds of consciousness. He had a divine consciousness and also a human consciousness. He was aware that He was both God and man. In the former, He could say: "I and my Father are one" (John 10:30); in the latter, He could say, "I thirst" (John 19:28).

Fourth, He was also one person with two wills. If Christ truly had two natures, then He must have had two wills, one human and the other divine. The Reformed theologian Shedd wrote: "Each nature, in order to be whole and entire, must have all of its essential elements. A human nature without voluntariness would be as defective as it would be without rationality." [11] Thus, in Christ, two natures or substances (*ousiai*) constitute one personal subsistence (*hupostasis*). Within the believer there often is the clash between the will of the old nature (sin nature) and the will of the new nature (implanted spiritual nature). Paul wrote: "For the flesh lusteth against the Spirit, and the Spirit against the flesh: and these are contrary the one to the other: so that ye cannot do the things that ye would" (Gal. 5:17). The Christian must decide whether he will yield to the dictates of the fleshly sin nature or to the direction of the Holy Spirit. Paul vividly described this struggle elsewhere:

For that which I do I allow not: for what I would, that do I not; but what I hate, that do I.

If then I do that which I would not, I consent unto the law that it is good.

Now then it is no more I that do it, but sin that dwelleth in me.

For I know that in me (that is, in my flesh,) dwelleth no good thing: for to will is present with me; but how to perform that which is good I find not.

For the good that I would I do not: but the evil which I would not, that I do.

Now if I do that I would not, it is no more I that do it, but sin that dwelleth in me.

I find then a law, that, when I would do good, evil is present with me.

For I delight in the law of God after the inward man:

But I see another law in my members warring against the law of my mind, and bringing me into captivity to the law of sin which is in my members (Rom. 7:15–23).

Paul had this struggle. Peter did, and so has every saint in every generation since creation. However, Jesus Christ never had this conflict of wills. He never had to cry out: "O wretched man that I am! who shall deliver me from the body of this death?" (Rom. 7:24). His human will and His divine will were in perfect harmony. As Shedd stated: "If the human will acts, the divine will submits and coacts. This is the humiliation of the divine. If the divine will acts, the human will submits and coacts. This is the exaltation of the human. One and the same Christ, therefore, performs the divine or the human action, as the case may be, although each action is wrought in accordance with the distinctive qualities of the will that corresponds with it, and takes the lead in it . . . . Thus, in any agency of the God-man, although there are two wills concerned in it, a divine and a human, there is but one resulting action." [12] Not only did Christ's divine and human wills work together in perfect and total union, but also, He always willed to do the Father's will. At the incarnation, He said: "Lo, I come (in the volume of the book it is written of me,) to do thy will, O God" (Heb. 10:7). In His earthly ministry, He claimed: "for I do always those things that please him." (John 8:29). In His anticipation of the crucifixion, He prayed: "O my Father, if it be possible, let this cup pass from me: nevertheless not as I will, but as thou wilt" (Matt. 26:39).

Fifth, the two natures were not altered by their union within the one person of Christ. Walvoord explained: "Just as any essence is composed of the sum of its attributes and their relationship, a change of any attribute would necessarily involve a change in essence. For instance, infinity cannot be transferred to finity; mind cannot be transferred to matter; God cannot be transferred to man, or vice versa. To rob the divine nature of God of a single attribute would destroy His deity, and to rob man of a single human attribute would result in destruction of a true humanity. It is for this reason that the two natures of Christ cannot lose or transfer a single attribute." [13] God is immutable; He does not change in His essence or character (Mal. 3:6; James 1:17). Christ is also "the same yesterday, and today, and forever" (Heb. 13:18). At the virgin conception, there was no diminishing of either nature nor was there any exchange of properties from one nature to the other. In maintaining their view on the ubiquity of Christ, the Lutherans have wrongly transferred the divine attribute of omnipresence to the human body of Jesus. They claim that Christ is everywhere present in a flesh and bone body. This not only defies human imagination, but it also contradicts the Scriptural delineation of a human nature.

How can Christ be both with and in believers today (Matt. 28:18; Col. 1:27) and at the same time be resident in the third heaven? His possession of the divine nature permits Him to be omnipresent, but His acquisition of a human nature limits His manifested presence to one place at one time. His human nature does not indwell the believer. And yet, He is one person. *He* is in heaven and still *He* is with the believer and in him. No one would say that the human body thinks or that the human soul walks; rather, a man thinks and walks. So it is with the theanthropic person of Christ. It is wrong to say that His divine nature suffered or that His human nature walked on the water. It is theologically correct to say that He walked on the sea and that He died. Although the action may have manifested one nature as against the other, yet all actions were the deeds of one person.

Sixth, both divine and human characteristics and deeds may be attributed to His person under any of His names whether they be divine or human titles. It is proper to say that Jesus was the redeemer even though no human could save another. It is also correct to state that the Son of God thirsted although God doesn't have to drink to sustain Himself. Human attributes were ascribed to Him under a divine title: Emmanuel, the Son of God, was born (Matt. 1:23; Luke 1:35) and the Lord of glory was crucified (1 Cor. 2:8). On the opposite side, divine attributes were ascribed to Him under a human title: the Son of man ascended to heaven where He was before (John 6:62) and the slain Lamb was worthy to receive power, riches, wisdom, strength, honor, glory, and blessing (Rev. 5:12).

Seventh, the union of the two natures was not changed by Christ's death, burial, resurrection, and ascension and will remain unaltered throughout eternity. At the cross, an immaterial human death took place. His real self separated from the material body. As the lifeless body hung on the cross and subsequently was placed into the tomb, the immaterial Jesus descended into Hades or hell to await the moment of resurrection (Acts 2:27 cf. 2:30–31). What occurred was the separation of the divine person with His divine nature and His human immaterial nature (soul and spirit) from the human body. There was no separation of the divine nature from the human nature at the crucifixion. He was no less human after His death than any normal individual is after his death. Human death occurs when the immaterial self, consisting of soul and spirit, is separated from the material body. Although the body may be in the ground, he as a human person is either in heaven or in hell. At the resurrection, Christ's real self, including His divine nature and His immaterial human nature, were joined to a new immortal, incorruptible body forever. At this time, His human nature did not gain the attributes of the divine nature. Just as we humans will not gain omniscience, omnipotence, or omnipresence at our resurrection, neither did the attributes of Christ's divine nature transfer to His human nature at His resurrection. Although the resurrection body will not need to eat or to drink to sustain itself, it may do so, not because it will have achieved the status of deity, but because that is one of the inherent qualities of the resurrected, human body.

Eighth, both natures could be manifested during a single event. When the woman with an issue of blood received healing by touching the hem of Jesus' garment, He knew that power had gone out of Him, and yet He said: "Who touched my clothes?" (Mark 5:30). The omniscience of His divine nature was balanced by the limited, uninformed knowledge of His human intellect. One morning, hungry, "seeing a fig tree afar off having leaves, he came, if haply he might find any thing thereon: and when he came to it, he found nothing but leaves; for the time of figs was not yet" (Mark 11:13). His approach to the fig tree reflected the natural ignorance of His human mind, but His cursing of the tree revealed His omnipotence and omniscience: "No man eat fruit of thee hereafter for ever" (Mark 11:14). When Jesus came to Bethany after the death of Lazarus, He said: "Where have ye laid him? They said unto him, Lord, come and see" (John 11:34). In His uninformed human intellect, Jesus did not know the site of Lazarus' burial, but when He came to the tomb, He raised Lazarus out of death, a demonstration of His omnipotence. Concerning His second advent, Jesus said: "But of that day and that hour knoweth no man, no, not the angels which are in heaven, neither the Son, but the Father" (Mark 13:32). Many evangelicals have become troubled over this assertion, but they need not be. The omniscience of His divine nature knew, but Jesus chose not to exercise this attribute. Rather, in His human comprehension He did not know the exact hour of His return because it had not been revealed to Him by the Father. Some have claimed that this is an *official* ignorance. Augustine, the great church father, wrote: "Christ as the Mediator was not authorized, at that time, to give information respecting the time of the final judgment." Although that explanation seems plausible, no one in an attempt to defend Christ's deity should deny His true humanity. Jesus did increase in wisdom (Luke 2:52) and He did learn obedience (Heb. 5:8). Lack of knowledge should not be construed as sin or as human imperfection. No one expects a one-year-old infant to work algebra problems. Christ, at His virgin conception, gained a human intellect that had to learn step by step. That sameness of human nature should not be denied to Him. He was both divine *and* human.

13 The Sinlessness Of Jesus

Like begets like. Dogs beget dogs; cats beget cats; and sinful men beget sinful men. Job was correct when he raised this rhetorical question: "Who can bring a clean thing out of an unclean? not one" (Job 14:4). Later Bildad agreed:

How then can man be justified with God? or how can he be clean that is born of a woman?
Behold even to the moon, and it shineth not; yea, the stars are not pure in his sight.
How much less man, that is a worm? and the son of man, which is a worm (Job 25:4–6)?

David's confession is the testimony of every man: "Behold, I was shapen in iniquity; and in sin did my mother conceive me" (Ps. 51:5). All men genetically sinned and died spiritually in Adam (Rom. 5:12). At the moment of conception, the parents pass on to their offspring a sin nature, a tendency to do that which is morally wrong and contrary to the character of God. Very early in life, the child manifests the fruit of its rebellious nature with its "No, No!" No one needs to teach the child how and when to disobey; he will do it automatically. He sins because he is a sinner, not vice versa. An apple tree is an apple tree long before it bears apples; the fruit always manifests the root or the nature. If any person denies the existence of his own sin nature or the reality of his personal acts and attitudes of sin, he is simply self-deluded (1 John 1:8–10). The most moral of all men, like Nicodemus and Paul, need to have a life-transforming experience of spiritual regeneration (cf. John 3:3; Phil. 3:4–9). Before an absolutely holy God, they must all admit: "But we are all as an unclean thing, and all our righteousnesses are as filthy rags" (Isa. 64:6).

Since Jesus Christ was born of a woman, how could He escape from being a sinner in nature and sinful in practice? Didn't Mary pass on to Him a sinful tendency at the conception? If she didn't, doesn't that make Him either more than human or less than a real man? Someone once wrote: "To err is human." Shouldn't moral error therefore be expected of Him? That axiom, first of all, is based upon human observation, not upon Scriptural teaching. Sinning is not a necessary part of human nature. God created Adam and Eve as a perfect man and woman. They were totally human, and yet, they had no sin nature, had thought no evil ideas, and had done no wicked works. They became sinners when they deliberately disobeyed God and ate the forbidden fruit. That sin nature which they acquired was then passed from generation to generation throughout the history of mankind.

The Scriptures definitely teach that Jesus Christ was both totally human and free from sinful contamination. Paul said that He "knew no sin" (2 Cor. 5:21). The author of Hebrews stated that He "was in all points tempted like as we are, yet without sin" (Heb. 4:15). Peter wrote that He "did no sin, neither was guile found in his mouth" (1 Peter 2:22). John claimed that "in him is no sin" (1 John 3:5). Christ Himself challenged His enemies: "Which of you convinceth me of sin?" (John 8:46). These clear declarations are supported by other lines of evidence. The angel Gabriel told Mary that her child would be "that holy thing" (Luke 1:35). Although Christ came to save sinners and even associated with them much to the consternation of the Pharisees, yet He was still "separate from sinners" (Heb. 7:26). Paul warned believers that "evil communications corrupt good manners" (1 Cor. 15:33), but Jesus was never defiled by His contacts with evil men. He remained "undefiled" (Heb. 7:26), "without blemish and without spot" (1 Peter 1:19). The tongue is the most difficult member of the body to control (James 3:2, 8), and yet, Jesus never had an untimely "slip of the lip." Even His critics could not force Him into a verbal error (cf. Matt. 22:15). Even during His trial and execution as a common criminal, He was declared to be innocent eleven times: by Judas (Matt. 27:4); by Pilate six times (in order John 18:38; Luke 23:14; 23:22; John 19:4; 19:6; Matt. 27:24); by Herod Antipas (Luke 23:15); by the wife of

Pilate (Matt. 27:19); by the repentant thief (Luke 23:41); and by the Roman centurion (Matt. 27:54).

Jesus claimed that He did "always those things that please" the Father (John 8:29) and that He had kept His Father's commandments (John 15:10). That is either "brag or fact." Even late in his life Paul had to admit that He had not done all that God wanted Him to do and that He had not yet become that person God wanted him to be (Phil. 3:12–14). Christ calmly and humbly asserted His total obedience. He further said that "the prince of this world cometh, and hath nothing in me" (John 14:30). Satan is "the god of this world" (2 Cor. 4:4), the spiritual father of all unsaved men. All men born into this world are spiritually "dead in trespasses and sins" and walk "according to the prince of the power of the air, the spirit that now worketh in the children of disobedience" (Eph. 2:1–2). All men, if they were honest with themselves, would admit with Paul: ". . . we all had our conversation [manner of living] in times past in the lusts of our flesh, fulfilling the desires of the flesh and of the mind; and were by nature the children of wrath, even as others" (Eph. 2:3). According to Jesus, Satan had no such control over Him. Jesus never gave His own personal testimony about His spiritual conversion. He taught others to view themselves as sinners, but He never admitted to any personal sin or moral guilt. He taught the disciples to pray for their forgiveness and for the spiritual needs of others, but He never requested such prayer for Himself. In His prayers and sermons, He never included Himself as a mutual recipient of the blessings and the admonitions. He never apologized. On the stormy sea, the disciples questioned the concern of the sleeping Jesus, but He blamed their fear upon their lack of faith in His word and in His presence (Mark 4:38 cf. 4:40). Mary and Joseph asked the twelve-year-old Jesus after five days of separation: "Son, why hast thou thus dealt with us?" (Luke 2:48). They put the blame on Him, but He never admitted that He was sorry for causing them such anxiety and inconvenience. Rather, He said: "How is it that ye sought me? Wist [know] ye not that I must be about my Father's business?" (Luke 2:49). According to Jesus, they were at fault. They failed to understand His person and His mission. Furthermore, there is no Biblical indication that Jesus ever offered an animal sacrifice at the Jewish temple. God built within the moral, civil, and ceremonial laws that He gave to Israel through Moses a system of sacrifices because He knew that no man was capable of keeping all of the law all of the time. Christ taught in the temple, drove the religious merchants from the temple, but never offered a sacrifice there because He had no sin for which to seek atonement. In His life, He totally fulfilled the law.

Could Jesus be sinless and yet possess a sin nature transmitted by Mary? If this had been possible, He would have still been viewed as a sinner before God. The sinlessness of Christ must be based upon the absence of any sin nature in Him. Karl Barth, the European existential theologian, in his *Credo* claimed that the "sin-inheritance" came through the male parent only. Some evangelicals have also accepted this position, but it doesn't really solve the problem of Mary's relationship to Jesus. Whatever Mary conceived, naturally or supernaturally, would bear her likeness. This would include not only her humanity but also her sinful nature. The relationship of physical characteristics and mental capacities between parent and child is reflected in the transmission of genes and chromosomes, both dominant and recessive. However, the sin nature is not contained within a gene or a chromosome. A child will not be a murderer just because his parents were. The sin nature involves a moral and spiritual transmission, not a material sequence. In such a transmission, only one parent is needed, but of course, apart from Christ's virgin conception, both parents have always been involved. It is too arbitrary to attribute His sinless humanity to the absence of human male fertilization. Schleiermacher strangely said that Christ "had an earthly father, but that by a supernatural operation on the embryo it was cleansed from original sin." [1] This view denied the historical reality of the virgin conception in its attempt to explain the unique sinlessness of the man Jesus. In so doing, it contradicted the testimony of Scripture. Why should the offspring of Joseph and Mary be given such preferential treatment? Would not Schleiermacher's Jesus later succumb to the onslaughts of Satan even as the innocent Adam did?

As the eternal God the Son, Jesus Christ was naturally holy and sinless before His incarnation. However, to gain a sinless human nature, the virgin birth had to take place. The popular apologist

Walter Martin differed, however: "Some Christians are led astray here because they are led into the fallacy that unless Christ was virgin born He could not have been sinless. Such a view would limit the omnipotence of God 'for with God all things are possible.' The answer, of course, is not that God was limited to the Virgin Birth to actuate the incarnation but that He decreed that the Virgin Birth would be the *means* of its realization." [2] The incarnation could not have occurred through the conception of two human parents even if God prevented the sin nature from being transmitted to the offspring; such a child could only be human. If God had created a special human nature which Christ could join to His divine nature, a theanthropic person would have resulted, but there would have been no direct, relevant relationship to the Jewish nation and to the human race. Could Jesus be the legal son of David without being the physical seed of David? Once the incarnation of God the Son was determined in the eternal plan, the means became limited. It had to be through the virgin conception to account for the many complex purposes associated with it.

The angel said to Mary: "The Holy Ghost shall come upon thee, and the power of the Highest shall overshadow thee: therefore also that holy thing which shall be born of thee shall be called the Son of God" (Luke 1:35). At the critical moment of conception, when God the Son entered into the unfertilized egg of Mary, she was prevented by the Spirit of God from passing to the living fetus her sin nature. The virgin conception, pregnancy, and birth manifest a sacred, sanctified mystery. No man knows all that happened in that historic moment, but the fact that Jesus Christ possessed two natures *apart from sin* argues back to the virgin conception.

The Bible says that Christ "was in all points tempted like as we are, yet without sin" (Heb. 4:15). Because Christ "himself hath suffered being tempted, he is able to succour them that are tempted" (Heb. 2:18). However, James wrote that "God cannot be tempted with evil" (James 1:13). How then could Jesus Christ, who was God manifest in the flesh, be tempted? Matthew gave this record of His temptation:

Then was Jesus led up of the spirit into the wilderness to be tempted of the devil.

And when he had fasted forty days and forty nights, he was afterward an hungered.

And when the tempter came to him, he said, If thou be the Son of God, command that these stones be made bread.

But he answered and said, It is written, Man shall not live by bread alone, but by every word that proceedeth out of the mouth of God.

Then the devil taketh him up into the holy city, and setteth him on a pinnacle of the temple,

And saith unto him, If thou be the Son of God, cast thyself down: for it is written, He shall give his angels charge concerning thee: and in their hands they shall bear thee up, lest at any time thou dash thy foot against a stone.

Jesus said unto him, It is written again. Thou shalt not tempt the Lord thy God.

Again, the devil taketh him up into an exceeding high mountain, and showeth him all the kingdoms of the world, and the glory of them,

And saith unto him, All these things will I give thee, if thou wilt fall down and worship me.

Then saith Jesus unto him, Get thee hence, Satan: for it is written, Thou shalt worship the Lord thy God, and him only shalt thou serve.

Then the devil leaveth him, and, behold, angels came and ministered unto him (Matt. 4:1–11).

Some observations need to be made about this passage. First, it was the will of God for Jesus to be tempted. He was led by the Holy Spirit into this experience (4:1 cf Mark 1:12, "the Spirit driveth him forth"). Since God does not tempt anyone to evil (James 1:13), this solicitation came from Satan. Second, Jesus was "full of the Holy Spirit" at the time of His temptation (Luke 4:1). Third, this threefold solicitation was actually just the climax to forty days of satanic temptation (Mark 1:13; Luke 4:2). Fourth, the temptation in principle was the same encountered by Eve and by every man. The three major classifications of sinful solicitation are the lust of the flesh, the lust of the eyes, and the pride of life (1 John 2:16). When Eve saw "that the tree was good for food [lust of the flesh], and that it was pleasant to the eyes [lust of the eyes], and a tree to be desired to make one wise [pride of life], she took of the fruit thereof, and did eat, and gave also unto her husband with her; and he did eat" (Gen. 3:6). In comparison, Jesus was tempted to satisfy His hungry stomach (lust of the flesh), to be caught miraculously by the angels (pride of life), and to worship Satan after seeing and being offered the world's kingdoms (lust of the eyes). He was literally "in all points" tempted as we are. Fifth, in response to each solicitation, Jesus completely obeyed the written Word of God. The Psalmist wrote: "Thy word have I hid in mine heart, that I might not sin against thee" (Ps. 119:11). Jesus was the personification of the truth of that verse. He was totally conscious of and submissive to every precept of divine revelation. Sixth, from the standpoint of circumstances, Jesus should have yielded to the satanic pressure whereas Adam should have been victorious. Adam lived in the Garden of Eden; Jesus was in the wilderness. Adam was full with much food available; Jesus was hungry with only stones to be seen. However, Jesus resisted, but Adam succumbed. Seventh, Satan recognized the dual natures of Christ. Twice he said to Jesus: "If thou be the Son of God" (Matt. 4:3, 6). At first glance, this phrase may seem to indicate that Satan was doubting the deity of Christ, but actually he was affirming it. The Greek text reads *ei huios ei tou theou.* He literally meant "If it is a fact that you are the Son of God, and I believe that you are, then you have the power in yourself to turn stone into bread to meet the physical needs of your human nature. Why don't you do it?" He wanted Christ to act independently as He had done in His preincarnate past. Rather, Jesus knew that *as man* He had to act in total dependence upon the will of God. Finally, because He experienced real human temptation, He is able to sympathize with all men in their temptations or tests, but *not* in their sins. Some men break under little pressure; others require great influence to yield, but Christ endured one hundred percent of Satan's very best strategy. In a sense, no human has ever been tempted like He was. He knows what temptation is really all about.

Jesus did not sin, but could he have sinned? Whale, a theological liberal, wrote: "We cannot conceive that Christ in the wilderness was truly pure unless we also conceive that He was able to sin, and *that he even desired to sin,* but did not [italics mine]."[3] Where in the Bible does it say or even imply that Jesus *desired* to sin? Whale failed to distinguish between a sin nature and a human nature and also between a sin nature and a human nature that is joined to a divine nature within one person. A contrast must be made between ability and desire; they are not the same.

Evangelical theologians have debated whether Christ was able not to sin (*posse non peccare*) or not able to sin (*non posse peccare*). Adam was created with an ability not to sin, but he chose deliberately to sin. Thereafter, he along with his descendants were *not* able *not* to sin (Eccles. 7:20). They were unable to keep themselves from sinning. Did Christ only have the original Adamic capacity? If so, then His sinlessness rested upon the obedience of His human will. The lack of ability to sin is a prerogative of the divine essence. Taken by themselves, the divine nature within the person of Christ was both intemptable and impeccable (Heb. 6:18; James 1:13) whereas the human nature was both temptable and peccable. Unfortunately, the debate reflects a lack of balance between the two natures. When Christ is viewed from the standpoint of His human nature, then proponents say that He was able not to sin. When He is viewed from the stance of His divine nature, then advocates state that Jesus was not able to sin. Paradoxically, both positions are right and wrong at the same time. Once the virgin conception occurred, the two natures were forever joined into one person. The question of Christ's sinlessness must really be viewed from the constitution of His theanthropic person. Shedd argued: "When these two natures are *united* in one theanthropic person, as they are in the incarnation, the divine determines and controls the human, not the human the divine." [4] Holiness is an essential part of divine immutability. God is holy, and therefore, He can't sin. That same nature belonged to Jesus Christ. To say that He could sin violates both His holiness and His unchangeableness. Shedd added: "Consequently, Christ while having a peccable human *nature* in his constitution, was an impeccable *person*. Impeccability characterizes the God-man as a totality, while peccability is a property of his humanity." [5] His sinlessness must be viewed from the result of the union of the two natures rather than from the perspective of each respective nature. Using the illustration of a wire (human nature) and an iron bar (divine nature), Shedd concluded: "An iron wire by itself can be bent and broken in a man's hand; but when the wire is welded into an iron bar, it can no longer be so bent and broken." [6]

Some have argued that if Christ was unable to respond to the satanic solicitations, then the temptation was not genuine. However, an army that can't be conquered can still be attacked. Satan was sincere when he tempted Jesus. The Savior did have a tempt-able human nature, but He could not yield because He was one person with a perfect union between His innate divine nature and His acquired human nature. Joseph Stump in *The Christian Faith* rightly observed: "Temptation is literally a testing, to see whether the tested one will choose God's service or not. This does not necessarily imply the possibility of a failure to stand the test. Gold may be tested as well as dross. And gold can never fail to stand the test. Theoretically, that is, as long as we do not know that the metal in question is gold, there may be the possibility in our minds that it will fail when put to the proof. But actually there is no such possibility." [7] The divine person of the Son of God was definitely "gold" even though to men He appeared to be like them, "in the likeness of sinful flesh" (Rom. 8:3).

Perhaps an analogy can be drawn from the production of the written Word of God. The forty authors of the sixty-six books were normal human beings possessing a sin nature. Whatever they did in the natural realm was finite and fallible. If the Bible is simply viewed as a human composition, then one would expect to find in it errors of history, chronology, geography, and theology. However, the Biblical writers did not write the Scriptures all by themselves. They did not originate the idea of a Biblical canon nor did they create the contents. Peter wrote: "For the prophecy came not in old time by the will of man: but holy men of God spake as they were moved by the Holy Ghost" (2 Peter 1:21). Just as the wind drives a sailing vessel so the Spirit provided the dynamic energy and the guidance for the Biblical writers. Paul wrote that "all scripture is given by inspiration of God" (2 Tim. 3:16). The last six words are the translation of one Greek word *theopneustos*. Literally, it means "breathed out by God." This does not mean that the authors wrote what they pleased and that God subse-quently breathed into their writings divine authority. Rather, what man wrote and what God said are one and the same (cf. Acts 28:25). God had providentially prepared the writers' life experi-ences so that their personalities including their distinctive methods of written communication were exactly the way God wanted them to be at the moment of writing. At the critical moment when the pen struck the paper, God so superintended them by the Holy

Spirit that they wrote exactly what God wanted them to write, leaving out nothing and adding nothing. They used their vocabularies and their styles of writing. They contributed a human character to the Scriptures, but they were prevented from passing on to the written product any errors. The Bible, therefore, is God's Word. It is one book with both a divine and a human nature. *So* it happened at the critical moment of conception within the womb of Mary. She had been providentially prepared and selected by God to be the channel through whom God's personal revelation would come. When she conceived, she passed on her human nature to the theanthropic person, but she was prevented by the Holy Spirit from transmitting a sin nature. The end result was that Jesus Christ was one person with two natures apart from sin and human flaw. The written Word of God mirrors the living Word of God. If Christ had not been virgin born under the overshadowing ministry of the Holy Spirit, then He could never have been free from the sinful taint that mars every human soul.

14 The Problem of The Creeds

How could the concept of the incarnation with the resultant hypostatic union of the two natures in Christ be put into a doctrinal or creedal confession? Creeds are not the basis of faith and practice; the Scriptures are. And yet, Christians have desired to express the teaching of Scripture in a doctrinal statement in order to express their beliefs, to define the limits of their church fellowship, and to test heretical thinking.

Early councils were careful about the way they expressed their convictions. They wanted to avoid erroneous theological language and concepts. Berkhof observed that the early church accepted doctrine "not because it had a complete understanding of the mystery, but because it clearly saw in it a mystery revealed by the Word of God. [1] They attempted to bring together all the salient passages into one embracing statement.

The earliest creedal statement is an old Roman baptismal confession. Machen wrote: "The Roman confession, which was written originally in Greek, must be dated at least as early as A.D. 200, because it is the ancestor not only of our Gallican creed [Apostles' Creed], but also of the many creeds used in various parts of the Western church." [2] The relevant phrase was "born of the Holy Ghost and the virgin Mary." The texts differ as to whether the word "of" was *ek* ("out of") or *dia* ("through"), but in either case, the virgin birth was clearly stated.

The early centuries of the Christian church were largely a struggle for survival in the midst of the Roman imperial persecutions. Once the Edict of Toleration was issued by the emperor Constantine, attention had to be given to theological matters. Many false teachings had gone unchecked and now had to be repudiated. The

Nicene Creed, developed about A.D. 325, marked out the deity of Jesus Christ as one of the doctrinal standards of the church:

And we believe in one Lord Jesus Christ, the only-begotten Son of God, begotten of the Father before all worlds; Light of Light, very God of very God, begotten not made, being of one substance with the Father; by whom all things were made; who, for us men, and for our salvation, came down from heaven and was incarnate by the Holy Ghost of the Virgin Mary, and was made man.

This creed was enlarged in A.D. 381 at Constantinople. Both declared that Jesus Christ was God and that He became man through the virgin birth. They made a clear distinction between "begotten" and "made" with the latter denoting an origin in time whereas the former referred to an eternal relationship. They denied the Arian concept that Christ was a created or a "made" angel.

The Council of Chalcedon (A.D. 451) focused on the person of Christ after His incarnation:

. . . one and the same Son, our Lord Jesus Christ, at once complete in Godhead and complete in manhood, truly God and truly man, consisting also of a reasonable soul and body; of one substance with the Father as regards his Godhead, and at the same time of one substance with us as regards his manhood; like us in all respects, apart from sin; as regards his Godhead, begotten of the Father before the ages, but yet as regards his manhood begotten, for us men and for our salvation, of Mary the Virgin . . . .

It further stated that He had "two natures, without confusion, without change, without division, without separation."

The popular Apostles' Creed, produced in the fifth or sixth century in Gaul, was based upon the old Roman baptismal confession. As expressed today, it states: "I believe in God the Father Almighty, Maker of Heaven and Earth; and in Jesus Christ, His only Son, our Lord, conceived by the Holy Ghost, born of the Virgin Mary, suffered under Pontius Pilate, was crucified, dead, and buried: descended into hell, on the third day He rose again from the dead; He ascended into heaven and sits on the right hand of God from whence He shall come to judge the quick and the dead, I believe in the Holy Ghost, the holy catholic church; the communion of saints, the forgiveness of sins, the resurrection of the body and the life everlasting." Many denominational churches recite this creed every Sunday, but to a large number of the clergy and the laity, they are only hollow words. Even demons admitted with their lips the deity of Christ; therefore, mere verbal assent is not equivalent to a heart conviction. Churches should scrutinize ministerial candidates carefully to discover whether the men *in fact* accept the *literal* incarnation via the *literal* virgin birth.

The Reformed faith is expressed in the Second Helvetic Confession:

We acknowledge, therefore, that there be in one and the same Jesus our Lord two natures—the divine and the human nature; and we say that these are so conjoined or united that they are not swallowed up, confounded, or mingled together, but rather united or joined together in one person (the properties of each being safe and remaining still), so that we do worship one Christ, our Lord, and not two. . . . Therefore we do not think nor teach that the divine nature in Christ did suffer, or that Christ, according to His human nature, is yet in the world, and so in every place.

The latter sentence was designed to offset the Lutheran view of the ubiquity of Christ's human nature.

In the Westminster Shorter Catechism, the Presbyterian confession of faith, this question is asked: "How did Christ, being the Son of God, become man?" The answer was thus stated: "Christ, the Son of God, became man, by taking to Himself a true body and a reasonable (i.e., reasoning) soul, being conceived by the power of the Holy Ghost, in the womb of the Virgin Mary, and born of her, yet without sin."

These creedal statements have not been quoted just to fill up space. They indicate that the tradition of the church involves the acceptance of the deity of Jesus Christ, His incarnation, and His virgin birth. Now, did the church accept these as facts because they were facts or did they come to accept error as fact? If the latter, then the church has been built upon delusion. If the former, then those who deny the physical reality of the virgin birth have separated themselves from the mainstream of historic Christianity.

In the incarnation, Jesus Christ acquired a true humanity. He then had two natures, divine and human, perfectly joined together in His single person. And yet, He was sinless. The only way that these realities could have been accomplished was through a historic, physical virgin conception and birth.

15 Why Did God Become Man?

Why did God need to become man? And why was it necessary for Him to become incarnate through the virgin birth? The Scriptures give definite answers to these searching questions.

To Reveal God to Man

Since God is invisible (1 Tim. 1:17), how could anyone experience Him with the senses? Could He only be known rationally or intuitively? Was He unknowable to the human eye, ear, and hand? What is He like?

Everything that God does reveals something about Himself. He manifested Himself through His work of creation. David sang: "The heavens declare the glory of God; and the firmament showeth his handiwork" (Ps. 19:1). He later wrote: "I will praise thee; for I am fearfully and wonderfully made" (Ps. 139:14). The stars, the planets, the sky, the hills and mountains, the rivers and oceans, and our very physical bodies, were designed to reveal truth about God's character and being. Only the fool would deny the existence of God as he studies the world through the telescope or the microscope (Ps. 14:1). Paul stated that God's existence, His power, and His intelligence, can be known by every man through nature: "Because that which may be known of God is manifest in them; for God hath showed it unto them. For the invisible things of him from the creation of the world are clearly seen, being understood by the things that are made, even his eternal power and Godhead" (Rom. 1:19–20).

God has also revealed Himself through the image of God that forms an innate part of each individual. F. F. Bruce wrote: "It is because God made man in His own image that He could accurately reveal Himself in a human life." [1] In a sense, God is more like man than anyone or anything else; also, man is more like God than like the highest ape. Man is a moral, spirit personality because God is a moral, spirit personality.

Although man can learn about God from the observation of a flower, it would have been totally inadequate for God to have become a rose or a petunia in order to reveal Himself more fully to man. Neither could He have become a rock, a snowflake, or a tree. To reveal Himself totally, He had to become a man. And that is exactly what He did.

The book of Hebrews stated: "God, who at sundry times and in divers manners spake in times past unto the fathers by the prophets, Hath in these last days spoken unto us by his Son" (Heb. 1:1–2). There is no comparison between visions, dreams, theophanic manifestations and "the real thing," the incarnation. Only in Jesus Christ can one fully see the essence of God. Jesus Himself said to His disciples:

If ye had known me, ye should have known my Father also: and from henceforth ye know him, and have seen him.
Philip saith unto him, Lord, show us the Father, and it sufficeth us.
Jesus saith unto him, Have I been so long time with you, and yet hast thou not known me, Philip? he that hath seen me hath seen the Father; and how sayest thou then, Show us the Father?
Believest thou not that I am in the Father, and the Father in me? the words that I speak unto you I speak not of myself: but the Father that dwelleth in me, he doeth the works.
Believe me that I am in the Father, and the Father in me: or else believe me for the very works' sake (John 14:7–11).

Since the Father and the Son are one in essence, Christ could say that seeing Him and seeing the Father were the same. He is "the image of the invisible God" (Col. 1:15). John wrote: "No man hath seen God at any time; the only begotten Son, which is in the bosom of the Father, he hath declared him" (John 1:18). No one was or is capable of viewing God in His naked deity. Since God is omnipresent Spirit, how could anyone look upon Him in His divine essence? To know a person, that person must choose to reveal Himself. Personalities are not known like mere objects. The latter can be weighed, measured, and analyzed for chemical structure. A person, naturally, can be reduced statistically: five feet ten inches tall, 165 pounds, black hair, brown eyes, etc. However, just because that data is available, it cannot be said that the person under investigation is known. From mere observation, you cannot tell that he likes to wear sport clothes, to play golf and tennis, and to eat Polish sausage and cabbage rolls. He must tell you either orally or in written form or he may choose to do those things in front of you. Christ "declared" God to man. He exegeted (*exegesato*) the Father. He led the hidden God out into open view so that everyone could see what God was like. Is God emotional? Jesus wept at the tomb of Lazarus (John 11:35). Is God righteous? Jesus drove the money changers out of the temple courtyards. Is God only concerned about adults? Jesus desired the little children to be brought to Him (Matt. 18:1–10). Some things could be learned about God from an investigation into the created world, but God had to become man in order for man to come to know God as a warm, personal being, completely concerned about man's basic needs. Suppose that a man accidentally stepped on an ant. How could the man know how the living ants "felt" about the death of their comrade? How could the man express His sorrow and concern over what happened? If the man could become an ant, then he could experience ant "feelings." Thus, he could communicate to other ants in their "language" and "culture" his innermost concern.

God did become man to reveal Himself to man. In so doing, He could sympathize with human experiences, and men could view God in action. This event occurred when the virgin Mary conceived.

To Provide Redemption for Man

Job asked: "How then can man be justified with God?" (Job 25:4). Paul asked the opposite question: how can God remain just, true to His righteous character, and justify anyone? (cf. Rom. 3:26). God could not arbitrarily excuse the sin of man. The role of the judge is to "justify the righteous, and condemn the wicked" (Deut. 25:1). God could never declare a sinner to be righteous unless that sinner was first made righteous, but how could that be accomplished? Paul stated: "For he [Father] hath made him

[Son] to be sin for us, who knew no sin; that we might be made the righteousness of God in him" (2 Cor. 5:21). Isaiah wrote:

Surely he hath borne our griefs, and carried our sorrows: yet we did esteem him stricken, smitten of God, and afflicted.

But he was wounded for our transgressions, he was bruised for our iniquities: the chastisement of our peace was upon him; and with his stripes we are healed.

All we like sheep have gone astray; we have turned every one to his own way; and the Lord hath laid on him the iniquity of us all (Isa. 53:4–6).

Philip explained to the Ethiopian eunuch that this passage definitely referred to Jesus Christ (Acts 8:30–35).

A redemption price had to be paid, but who could make it? Only one deemed worthy by God the Father could provide the atonement. Job despaired: "Neither is there any daysman betwixt us, that might lay his hand upon us both" (Job 9:33). Eli, the old judge of Israel, wondered: "If one man sin against another, the judge shall judge him: but if a man sin against the Lord, who shall intreat for him?" (I Sam. 2:25). John wept because no one "in heaven, nor in earth, neither under the earth" was worthy to approach the Father (Rev. 5:1–4). However, John was told to stop weeping because the slain, resurrected Lamb of God, even Jesus Christ, could do it (Rev. 5:5–7). There had to be a mediator who could bring a holy God and a sinful human race together. His identification is obvious: "For there is one God, and one mediator between God and men, the man Christ Jesus" (1 Tim. 2:5). The only adequate mediator had to be both God and man and the only way that that end could be achieved was through a real incarnation. Boettner commented: "In his fallen condition man has neither the inclination nor the ability to redeem himself. All merely human works are defective and incapable of redeeming a single soul. Between the Holy God and sinful man there is an infinite gulf; and only through One who is Deity, who takes man's nature upon Himself and suffers and dies in his stead, thus giving infinite value and dignity to that suffering and death, can man's debt be paid." [2] A man in himself can bear the wrath of God, but he cannot bear it redemptively. Throughout eternity, finite man will suffer an eternal punishment for his sins against an infinite, eternal God. By becoming man, God the Son was able to suffer an infinite, eternal death in a moment of time.

The eternal decree involved redemption through the death and resurrection of God incarnate (2 Tim. 1:9). Christ knew that He came into the world to die (John 12:27). Peter said that Christ "was foreordained [to die] before the foundation of the world, but was manifest in these last times for you" (1 Peter 1:20). How could God who has self-existent life die? By His very nature, God can't die. To die, He had to become man because mortality is part of the human nature. The book of Hebrews stated: "Forasmuch them as the children are partakers of flesh and blood, he also himself likewise took part of the same; that through death he might destroy him that had the power of death, that is, the devil" (Heb. 2:14). If Jesus had been born through natural generation, He would have died like all mortals, but His death would not have had an infinite, eternal redemptive value. There had to be the incarnation of God the Son through the virgin conception to bring together into one person the two features necessary for redemption: human mortality and divine value.

From the killing of the substitute animal in the Garden of Eden to the crucifixion of Calvary, the divine principle of redemption has been: ". . . without shedding of blood [there] is no remission" (Heb. 9:22). God has no circulatory system: no heart, no arteries, no veins, and no blood. For God to shed blood, He had to become man. Paul declared that God purchased the church "with his own blood" (Acts 20:28). The Greek text reads *dia tou haimatos tou idiou,* literally "through the blood of His own." The last two words refer to Jesus Christ. The Father didn't have blood, but the Son did when He acquired a human body through the conception in the virgin's womb. Christ entered the heavenly tabernacle "by his own blood" (Heb. 9:12; same words as Acts 20:28). Only the blood of Christ could purge our consciences from dead works to serve the living God (Heb. 9:14).

The Gospel message includes both the death and the resurrection of Christ (1 Cor. 15:3–4). Salvation involves the deliverance of the body as well as the soul. No man could ever have received a new, immortal, incorruptible body unless Christ had been raised physically from the dead (1 Cor. 15:12-20). He had to have a real human body in order to die and also to be raised again.

His resurrection gave Him "an unchangeable priesthood. Wherefore he is able to save them to the uttermost that come unto God by him, seeing he ever liveth to make intercession for them" (Heb. 7:24–25). Christ's present ministry in heaven is only efficacious because He gained a true humanity. Earlier the author wrote: "Wherefore in all things it behoved him to be made like unto his brethren, that he might be a merciful and faithful high priest in things pertaining to God, to make reconciliation for the sins of the people" (Heb. 2:17). A priest represents man before God. To be man's priest, Christ had to become man; to stand forever before God, He also had to be divine.

In developing a holy life, Christians are instructed throughout the New Testament to look to Jesus Christ as their example. He is the model for humility and selflessness (John 13:13–15), the standard for altruism (Phil. 2:5–8), and the pattern for patient endurance (Heb. 12:2–4). He "suffered for us, leaving us an example, that ye should follow his steps: who did no sin, neither was guile found in his mouth: who, when he was reviled, reviled not again; when he suffered, he threatened not; but committed himself to him that judgeth righteously" (1 Peter 2:21–23). No man could follow His steps unless they were human steps!

To provide redemption for man from the penalty, power, and presence of sin, God the Son had to be virgin born to acquire a true humanity. No other method of incarnation would have secured the needed mediator and example.

To Complement the Messianic Program

Christ both privately and publicly declared that the Old Testament pointed to Him (Luke 24:27, 44; John 5:39, 46). From Genesis to Malachi, there are direct predictions of His person and work, plus typological and historical allusions to Him.[3] At no time did God reveal all the truth about the coming Messiah to any one individual or group. Rather, the Old Testament presentation of the Messiah must be seen as a jigsaw puzzle instead of as a portrait. Through various ages, God progressively disclosed one piece of the puzzle after another. With the completion of the Old Testament canon, the puzzle was complete and each piece could be seen in its relevance to the other pieces (predictions). The prediction of the Messiah's virgin birth, therefore, must not be viewed in isolation from all other prophetic Scriptures. It is a necessary part of the whole. A knowledge of the messianic program in the Old Testament, therefore, forms a necessary background against which the specific virgin birth prophecy can be studied.

After the sinful fall of Adam and Eve, God spoke to the satanic serpent: "And I will put enmity between thee and the woman, and between thy seed and her seed; it shall bruise thy head, and thou shalt bruise his heel" (Gen. 3:15). Identified as the proto-evangelium, many evangelicals claim that this verse directly refers to the virgin birth of Christ whereas others would state that the virgin birth is only implicit within the wording "her seed." Normally "seed" is related to the man, not to the woman. The choice of "her" rather than "his" or "their" must be considered seriously. There is a problem as to the identity of the woman. Was God referring to a literal woman like Eve or Mary or was this a figurative usage for the line of the women who would mother each male ancestor of Jesus who was genetically present in every generation? Perhaps it could have a double reference. In the book of Revelation, John observed:

And there appeared a great wonder in heaven; a woman clothed with the sun, and the moon under her feet, and upon her head a crown of twelve stars:
And she being with child cried, travailing in birth, and pained to be delivered. . . .

. . . and the dragon stood before the woman which was ready to be delivered, for to devour her child as soon as it was born.
And she brought forth a man child, who was to rule all nations with a rod of iron: and her child was caught up unto God, and to his throne.
And the woman fled into the wilderness . . . (Rev. 12:1–6).

The man child is definitely Christ. Although some Roman Catholics view the woman as Mary, she no doubt represents the messianic nation Israel. In one of Joseph's dreams, the sun represented Jacob, the moon represented Rachel, and the stars symbolized the twelve sons of Jacob whose names became the titles for the twelve tribes of the nation Israel (Gen. 37:9–10). There was to be a hatred between Satan and his human instruments and the providentially protected messianic line of male descendants that would be climaxed in the bruising or crucifixion of Jesus Christ. All of these were satanically inspired plots to destroy the human line of "her seed": the slaying of Abel by Cain; the attempt to kill all Jewish male babies by the Egyptian Pharaoh; the conspiracy of Haman to exterminate all Jews in the time of Esther; and the decree of Herod the Great to slay all Jewish male infants two years of age and under in the region around Bethlehem. Satan, however, was unsuccessful, and although Christ was bruised for our iniquities (Isa. 53:5), He conquered Satan (Heb. 2:14). The line of fertile women necessary to generate the human messiah reached its climax in Mary who, apart from male fertilization, gave birth to the Christ. A word of caution should be given here. Both her mother and brother said to Rebekah: ". . . let thy seed possess the gate of those which hate them" (Gen. 24:60). By Isaac, Rebekah gave birth to Esau and Jacob. Therefore "thy seed" did not teach or imply a virgin birth. It is a moot question whether "her seed" (Gen. 3:15) and "thy seed" (Gen. 24:60) should be regarded as analagous. The former was spoken by God, and the latter was declared by two human relatives, and that fact alone points out one great difference in the two passages.

The Messiah was to be a descendant of Seth (Gen. 5:3), Shem, the son of Noah (Gen. 9:26), Abraham (Gen. 12:1–3), Isaac (Gen. 26:4 cf. Rom. 9:7), Jacob (Gen. 35:9–15), Judah (Gen. 49:10), and David (2 Sam. 7:12–17). God promised Abraham that both in him and in his seed all families of the earth would be blessed (Gen. 12:3; 12:28). Repeated later to Jacob (Gen. 28:14), the promise not only involved the national seed or Israel but also the personal seed, namely Christ. Paul argued: "Now to Abraham and his seed were the promises made. He saith not, And to seeds, as of many; but as of one, and to thy seed, which is Christ" (Gal. 3:16). By the Spirit of God, Paul saw that the usage of the singular "seed" contained a hidden reference to Christ. Each messianic male descendant of Abraham could properly be designated as the singular "seed," and yet, Christ was genetically present in each one. The original promise given to Abraham had

to have its final fulfillment in Christ Himself. That is why the New
Testament opens with the words: "Jesus Christ, the son of David,
the son of Abraham" (Matt. 1:1).

In his final words, Jacob pronounced this blessing upon Judah:

> Judah, thou art he whom thy brethren shall praise: thy hand shall
> be in the neck of thine enemies; thy father's children shall bow down
> before thee.
> Judah is a lion's whelp: from the prey, my son, thou art gone up:
> he stooped down, he couched as a lion, and as an old lion; who shall
> rouse him up?
> The sceptre shall not depart from Judah, nor a lawgiver from
> between his feet, until Shiloh come; and unto him shall the gathering
> of the people be (Gen. 49:8–10).

Although the eleven brothers did not fall down before Judah himself, their descendants did prostrate themselves before David, the
first member of the tribe of Judah to reign as king. Genetically,
the descendants of the brothers *in* the brothers did bow before
both Judah and his posterity, including David and his greater son,
Jesus Christ. The word "Shiloh" means "to whom it is" (*she* =
whom; l = to; *oh* = him). According to Jacob, the sceptre or the
symbol of self-government would not depart from the tribe
of Judah until "he to whom it belongs" arrived. Since that govern-
mental concept ended with the destruction of Jerusalem by the
Romans (A.D. 70), "Shiloh" had to have come before that event.
He did in the person of Christ.

When the Jewish kingdom was first established, a member of
the tribe of Benjamin, Saul, was anointed as the first king. There
was a specific reason why the tribe of Judah was bypassed at
that time. Judah had unwittingly committed incest with his daugh-
ter-in-law and had impregnated her (Gen. 38). Moses later wrote:
"A bastard shall not enter into the congregation of the Lord; even
to his tenth generation shall he not enter into the congregation
of the Lord" (Deut. 23:2). From Judah to Jesse, the father of
David, were ten generations (Ruth 4:18–22). If the count started
with Judah, then Jesse who was an adult at the time of Saul's
coronation could not have reigned, but Jesse's son could. If the
count started with Judah's illegitimate son, Pharez, then David,

the tenth, could not have entered. However, the son of David, the messianic title applied to Christ, could.

The Messiah was to be a prophet (Deut. 18:15), a priest (1 Sam. 2:35), and a king (Ps. 24). In Israel, priests and kings could also be prophets, but no one could be both a priest and a king. Priests came out of the tribe of Levi and kings out of Judah. Jesus was "the Lion of the tribe of Judah" (Rev. 5:5) and became a priest according to the order of Melchisedec by divine appointment (Ps. 110:4 cf. Heb. 5:1–6).

The messianic Psalms implied the possibility of a virgin birth. A real human generation can be seen in these Davidic utterances: "But thou art he that took me out of the womb: thou didst make me hope when I was upon my mother's breasts. I was cast upon thee from the womb: thou art my God from my mother's belly" (Ps. 22:9–10). The absence of a human father may be detected in this declaration: "I am become a stranger unto my brethren, and an alien unto my mother's children" (Ps. 69:8). How could the messiah have a mother and brothers without having a father? Only through a virgin birth for Himself and a natural birth for His brothers by His mother and her husband, their father.

His birthplace was to be Bethlehem (Micah 5:2). Although David was born in that city, all subsequent kings of Judah were born in Jerusalem. He was to be anointed by the Spirit for His preaching and healing ministries (Ps. 2:2; Isa. 61:1–2). His activity was to be announced by a forerunner, later identified as Elijah (Isa. 40:3; Mal. 4:5). He was destined to suffer for the sins of His people (Ps. 22; Isa. 53). The time of His advent could be calculated (Dan. 9:24–27; Mal. 3:1). He had to come before the destruction of the Zerubbabel-Herod temple. As discussed in an earlier chapter, He also had to be God (Ps. 2:7; 110:1; Isa. 9:6).

16 Fulfilling Isaiah 7:14

After the angel explained to Joseph that Mary's pregnancy was caused by the activity of the Holy Spirit, Matthew commented: "Now all this was done that it might be fulfilled which was spoken of the Lord by the prophet, saying, Behold, a virgin shall be with child, and shall bring forth a son, and they shall call his name Emmanuel, which being interpreted is, God with us" (Matt. 1:22–23). The quoted Old Testament verse was: "Therefore the Lord himself shall give you a sign; Behold, a virgin shall conceive, and bear a son, and shall call his name Immanuel" (Isa. 7:14). Matthew definitely saw in Mary's pregnancy the fulfillment of the prophetic passage. However, liberals believe that the Gospel author misapplied that prophecy to Jesus as he did with subsequent ones (cf. Matt. 2:15). They deny both that Jesus was virgin born and that the Isaiah passage predicted or implied a virgin birth. To them, the prophecy had an immediate, historical fulfillment in Isaiah's own day. Some evangelical writers have even wondered whether a virgin birth was the intended sign. Herbert Wolf, a Wheaton College professor, wrote: "In an analogous manner Matthew selected Isa. 7:14 to describe the birth of Jesus. The language was perfectly suited to Matthew's purpose; and where he went beyond the normal interpretation, he clearly explained the circumstances." [1] Wolf cited the Egyptian residency of Jesus and the Herodian decree to slay male infants (2:15 cf. Hosea 11:1; 2:18 cf. Jer. 31:15) as other illustrations of Matthew's technique. However, it must be seen that the usage of the Old Testament by Matthew or any other New Testament author was not arbitrary or an expression of human ingenuity. When they claimed that an event fulfilled an Old Testament prophecy, they did so by the revealing, guiding ministry of the Holy

Spirit (John 14:26; 16:12–15). The question doesn't really center around Matthew's purpose; it focuses upon the primary intent of Isaiah 7:14. Did God reveal through Isaiah the virgin conception and birth as the means of the incarnation of His Son or did He just announce a natural birth that would have significance in the eighth century b.c. and that could be used typically or analogically of the birth of Jesus? The same Spirit of God that guided Isaiah to write also superintended the composition of Matthew. The fulfillment must match the prophecy perfectly.

The total absence of sexual intimacies is clearly seen in the word "virgin" *(parthenos)*. Jesus Himself used this word three times in the parable of the ten virgins (Matt. 25:1, 7, 11). Luke used it twice of Mary (Luke 1:27) and of Philip's four prophetic daughters (Acts 21:9). Paul made a difference between a wife and a virgin (1 Cor. 7:34 cf. 7:25, 28, 36, 37). Spiritual faithfulness was equated to chaste virginity (2 Cor. 11:2). The word was even descriptive of men who had no sexual relationships with women and who were totally yielded to God (Rev. 14:14). Since sexual abstinence is essential to the meaning of *parthenos,* then not only was Mary a virgin, but the divine intent of Isaiah 7:14 involved true virginity. The best commentary upon the Old Testament is the New Testament; therefore, the Christian must view the prophecy through its fulfillment in Christ. The clear interpretation of Matthew 1:22–23 should explain whatever ambiguity one might find in Isaiah 7:14. This is the proper order of Christian exegesis.

The historical background of Isaiah's prophecy is most interesting. Rezin, the king of Syria, and Pekah, the king of the split nation Israel, had formed a military alliance against Ahaz, the king of Judah (Isa. 7:1–2a). Both Ahaz and Judah became frightened over this imminent threat (Isa. 7:2). God then instructed Isaiah to take his son Shear-jashub and to meet Ahaz at the upper pool, a part of Jerusalem's water system (Isa. 7:3). The presence of Shear-jashub, whose name meant "a remnant shall return," was indicative of God's faithful protection. Isaiah then informed Ahaz that both the invasion and the conspiracy to unseat Ahaz from the throne would fail (Isa. 7:4–7). He further stated that both Syria and Israel would be destroyed within sixty-five years

(Isa. 7:8–9). Isaiah then gave this confirmation of the above announcements:

Moreover the Lord spake again unto Ahaz, saying,
Ask thee a sign of the Lord thy God; ask it either in the depth, or in the height above.
But Ahaz said, I will not ask, neither will I tempt the Lord.
And he said, Hear ye now, O house of David; Is it a small thing for you to weary men, but will ye weary my God also?
Therefore the Lord himself shall give you a sign; Behold, a virgin shall conceive, and bear a son, and shall call his name Immanuel.
Butter and honey shall he eat, that he may know to refuse the evil, and choose the good.
For before the child shall know to refuse the evil, and choose the good, the land that thou abhorrest shall be forsaken of both her kings (Isa. 7:10–16)

When God offered to authenticate the pronouncement with a miraculous sign, the wicked, unbelieving king hypocritically refused to ask for one and chose rather to put his confidence in a confederacy with Assyria (cf. 2 Chron. 28). God then gave to the entire royal family of David, not just to Ahaz, a sign of His own choice ("you" in 7:14 is plural). The full meaning of the sign centers around the relationship of 7:14 to 7:15–16. The latter two verses seem to refer to a child in Isaiah's day who would not reach the age of moral accountability before Rezin and Pekah had been killed. Thus, how could this child be virgin born in the same way that Jesus was? What therefore was the divine meaning of the virgin conception as given by Isaiah?

Casserley regarded the application of Isaiah 7:14 to the virgin birth of Jesus by early Christian apologists as an "exegetical mistake." [2] The *Jewish Encyclopedia* claimed that the passage could refer to the birth of a child to any woman and that the significance rested only in the time element needed to eliminate the Syrian-Israelite threat: "In connection with Isaiah's Messianic hope it remains to be observed that the "Immanuel" passage, Isa. vii. 14 . . . has . . . no Messianic import whatever. The name has reference merely to events of the immediate present." [3] According to the scholarly historian Edersheim, the Jews had a list of 456 passages that referred to the Messiah, but Isaiah 7:14

was not one of them.[4] In itself, this should not be misconstrued as an argument against a predicted virgin birth because even the prophets did not understand everything which was revealed to them or spoken or written by them (Dan. 12:8; 1 Peter 1:10–12). The relationship of the sufferings of Christ to His eternal reign even baffled the disciples.

Evangelical approaches to the passage have differed. Some see it as strictly messianic, a prediction only of the virgin birth of Jesus by Mary. Others view it as typically messianic with the mother and child of Isaiah's day serving as divinely intended types of Jesus and His virgin mother. Most contemporary authors however regard the passage as a good illustration of the hermeneutical law of double reference. To the third group, the virgin refers either to: the wife of Ahaz; the second wife of Isaiah; or to any virgin within the nation Judah. Thus, according to that approach, the son refers to: Hezekiah, the son of Ahaz; Maher-shalal-hash-baz, the son of Isaiah; an unknown son of Isaiah; or to any anonymous son of any young mother. The third group has found it difficult to identify accurately the historical mother and child. Gleason Archer, a noted Old Testament scholar and professor at Trinity Evangelical Divinity School, claimed in the *Wycliffe Bible Commentary* that the virgin referred to Isaiah's fiancee, the prophetess, and that the child born to that relationship (Maher-shalal-hash-baz) bore the symbolical name of Immanuel (Isa. 8:1–4 cf. 8:8, 18). Others regard the virgin to be the prophetess, the wife taken by Isaiah after the death of his first wife who was the mother of Shear-jashub, but they view the son to be a third son, not Maher-shalal-hash-baz. In either case, Isaiah did identify himself and his sons as signs and wonders for Israel (Isa. 8:18). They point out that the usage of the definite article with the noun "virgin" means that the woman was well known both to Ahaz and to Isaiah. In historical fulfillment, the son born to Isaiah and the prophetess ate the standard diet of those who lived in a devastated land (Isa. 7:15). Before he reached the age of twelve, both Syria and Israel fell to the Assyrian armies (Isa. 7:16). Because of Ahaz's unbelief, the Assyrians also afflicted Judah (Isa. 7:17). The subsequent conflict between Assyria and Egypt stripped the land of Judah economically (Isa. 7:18). Later, Sennacherib, "the razor," leveled most of the cities of Judah (Isa. 7:20).

In his study on the development of various interpretations of Isaiah 7:14, Edward Hindson remarked that all early evangelical writers were strictly messianic in their approach but that they changed to a double fulfillment approach when the liberals began to stress a mere historical fulfillment in Isaiah's day.[5] In recent years, Edward J. Young, the brilliant scholar of Westminster Theological Seminary, in his commentary *The Book of Isaiah* called for a return to the strict messianic position.

Young's warning should be heeded because no concession should be made to antisupernaturalistic liberal scholarship unnecessarily. However, the Scripture does contain within it unique double references. The two advents, separated by at least two thousand years, were predicted in the same verse (Isa. 61:2 cf. Luke 4:16–21). Even the messianic psalms (Ps. 22: 69) mixed references to the psalmist's own circumstances with predictive elements. Thus, the significance of Isaiah's announcement to his generation was the time element needed to eliminate Judah's enemies (Isa. 7:15–16). This "time clock" child of course had to be born, but his birth would be to a new virgin bride. The destruction of Israel and Syria would be an assurance that God was indeed with the house of David in His providential presence. Isaiah's generation read back into verse fourteen a normal birth situation in order to account for the fulfillment of the next two verses. However, the direct divine intent of the sign was to the virgin birth of God the Son who would be among His people in His personal presence. God gave a sign that applied not only to Ahaz's day but to all subsequent generations of the house of David. The promise of the virgin-born messiah who was to be God incarnate was to be that guarantee that Judah or the royal house of David would never be totally obliterated by any foreign power. As always, a knowledge of the divine plan for the future should relieve any anxiety in the present. Thus, only 7:14 referred to Christ whereas 7:15–16 looked at the "time clock" child. The latter had to be born of a virgin through male fertilization whereas Christ was to be born of a virgin without male parentage.

Critics have questioned whether the Hebrew word *almah* should have been translated as "virgin." They claim that if Isaiah wanted to describe pure virginity he would have used the word *bethulah*. This is one reason why both the Revised Standard Version and the New English Bible have "young woman" instead of "virgin" in their translations. To any reader, the phrase "young woman" does not connote the presence or the absence of virginity. However, the Jewish translators of the Hebrew Old Testament into the Greek Septuagint in the third century B.C. used *parthenos* as the exchange word for *almah*. In their minds, *almah* denoted pure virginity. Alva J. McClain, the late president of Grace Theological Seminary, criticized the RSV translators for their change of translation: ". . . if the word *virgin* was a possible translation of the Hebrew word, then there could be no valid reason for not leaving the word *virgin* in the verse, unless they were determined to exclude from the prophecy any reference to the birth of Christ." [6] It is difficult to question a person's motivation, but in this case, it must be done. Why did the RSV editors choose "young woman" over "virgin"?

G. B. Gray, the author of the Isaiah volume in the *International Critical Commentary* series (usually written from a liberal perspective) admitted: ". . . *almah* means a girl, or young woman, above the age of childhood and sexual immaturity . . . a person of the age at which sexual emotion awakens and becomes potent; it asserts neither virginity nor the lack of it; it is naturally in actual usage applied to women who were as a matter of fact certainly (Gn. 24:43; Ex. 2:8), or probably (Ca 1:3; 6:8; Ps. 68:26), virgins." [7] Merrill Unger, the noted Old Testament scholar and theologian of Dallas Theological Seminary, noted that *almah* meant a young woman of marriageable age, that the primary idea was not unspotted virginity, that it could take the meaning of "virgin," and that the fulfillment in Christ's birth (Matt. 1:23) required that meaning in Isaiah 7:14.[8] The alternatives are clear. If the intent of *almah* by Isaiah was "virgin," then the passage had to be messianic in primary purpose referring to the virgin Mary. Its secondary reference would of necessity had to refer to a virgin, second wife of Isaiah. If virginity were not denoted by *almah*, then the virgin birth of Jesus was not predicted by Isaiah. Its primary and only reference would then have to refer to either Ahaz's or Isaiah's present wives who were not virgins at that time.

The word *almah* is used only nine times in the Hebrew Old Testament (Gen. 24:43; Ex. 2:8; 1 Chron. 15:20; Ps. 46:1; 68:25; Prov. 30:19; Song of Sol. 1:3; 6:8; Isa. 7:14). George Lawlor, professor of Bible at Cedarville College, demonstrated in his book *Almah . . . Virgin or Young Woman?* that eight of the above passages (excluding Isaiah 7:14) requires a translation of pure virginity. Rebekah was known both as a *bethulah* and an *almah* before she became Isaac's wife (Gen. 24:16 [*bethulah*] cf. 24:43 [*almah*]). The Bible clearly stated: ". . . neither had any man known her" (Gen. 24:16). Miriam, the sister of Moses, was identified as a virgin ("maid"—KJV) when she encouraged Pharaoh's daughter to save the life of the infant Moses (Ex. 2:8). Since she died during the wilderness wanderings (Num. 20:1), she must have been approximately fifteen years old at the time of Moses' rescue. The *alamoth* (1 Chron. 15:20; Ps. 46:1 [in the psalm title]) were probably virgin woman singers equivalent to "the damsels playing with timbrels" (Ps. 68:25). The wonderful thing of "the way of a man with a maid" (Prov. 30:19) may have referred to the first "honeymoon" experience of a newly married couple although Lawlor believed that it described the seduction of a virgin by a forceful man.[9] The virgins that loved the kingly bridegroom were probably royal attendants found in most palaces (Song of Sol. 1:3; 6:8 cf, Esther 2:1–20 [*bethulah* attendants]). In the light of these eight passages, the usage of *almah* in Isaiah 7:14 most definitely refers to a virgin. It cannot be argued that *bethulah* would have provided a stronger word for virginity. In fact, *bethulah* in one instance may have connoted just the opposite impression: "Lament like a virgin girded with sackcloth for the husband of her youth" (Joel 1:8). This sounds like a married wife who has lost her husband although Unger believed that this spoke of the loss of a betrothed husband, not a married one.[10] The unsurpassed scholar and linguist of Princeton Theological Seminary of a past generation, Robert Dick Wilson, summarized the meaning of *almah* quite well: "Two conclusions from the evidence seem clear; first that *alma,* so far as is known, never means "young married woman"; and secondly since the presumption in common law was and is, that every *alma* is a virgin and virtuous, until she is proven not to be, we have a right to assume that Rebekah and the *alma* of Isa. vii. 14, and all other *almas* were virgin, until and unless it shall be proven that they were not." [11]

Could a mere human birth fulfill the offer of a sign either in the depth or in the height? At the time Isaiah met Ahaz there were many virgins about to be married and many sons about to be conceived and born. There could be a significance in the time lapse between their conception and their attainment of moral accountability, but what would be the importance of mentioning 7:14? The word for "sign," *'oth*, technically does not mean a miracle, but it was used to describe the miracles that God performed through Moses in Egypt (Num. 14:22; Deut. 11:3). Actually, Ahaz did not propose this sign; God did. Should not a sign given by God be expected to be supernatural in character? All of God's activities are marvellous, but a special sign would in itself be unique. The word *'oth* could refer to physical objects such as the sun, moon and stars (Gen. 1:14), the mark of Cain (Gen. 4:15), the banners used to indicate the various families of Israel (Num. 2:2), the scarlet line hanging out of Rahab's window (Josh. 2:12), and the memorial altar which marked the crossing of the Jordan River (Josh. 4:6). The word was also used of historical events such as the exodus from Egypt (Ex. 3:12), the double deaths of Hophni and Phinehas in the same day (1 Sam. 2:34), the emotional change in Saul when he met the prophets (1 Sam. 10:7), and the turning back of Hezekiah's sun dial ten degrees (2 Kings 10:8).

The sign was not that any virgin would conceive, but that *the* virgin would conceive. The definite article appears both in the Hebrew (*ha almah*; Isa. 7:14) and the Greek texts (*he parthenos;* Matt. 1:23). This means that God was not speaking about any young woman who was a virgin at that time. He had a specific virgin in mind, otherwise there would have been no need to employ the definite article. The Hebrew grammar in the verse is also significant. Matthew used the Greek future tenses ("shall conceive" and "shall bear") as used in the Greek Septuagint version. However, the Hebrew text conveys a different shade of meaning. J. A. Alexander remarked: "As to the form of the expression it will only be necessary further to remark that *harah* ["shall conceive"] is not a verb or participle, but a feminine adjective, signifying "pregnant," and here connected with an active participle ["bear"], to denote that the object is described as present to the prophet's view." [12] Literally, the verse reads: "Behold the pregnant virgin is bearing a son and she calls his name Immanuel." The sign is that the virgin is still a virgin both at the time she is pregnant and when she brings forth her son. How could this be? A virgin ceases to be a virgin when she has experienced her first sexual intimacy with a man. Quite possibly, she could be a virgin at the time she became pregnant, but she could never be called a virgin during the length of her pregnancy. No conception and pregnancy by the wife of either Ahaz or Isaiah could satisfy the technical meaning of this verse. Only the virgin birth of Jesus by Mary could fulfill the divine sign. Mary was a virgin at the time she became pregnant and yet her virginity was unbroken because no intercourse occurred. She remained a virgin throughout her pregnancy, and when she brought forth Jesus in Bethlehem, she was still a virgin. That event was indeed a supernatural *'oth*. Isaiah later confirmed that neither his son or that of Ahaz could fulfill the destiny of Immanuel:

> For unto us a child is born, unto us a son is given: and the government shall be upon his shoulder: and his name shall be called Wonderful, Counsellor, The mighty God, The everlasting Father, The Prince of Peace.
> Of the increase of his government and peace, there shall be no end, upon the throne of David, and upon his kingdom, to order it, and to establish it with judgment and with justice from henceforth even for ever. The zeal of the Lord of hosts will perform this (Isa. 9:6–7).

No historical fulfillment could be found for either 9:6–7 or 7:14. If Ahaz's generation applied 7:14 as well as 7:15–16 to their day and derived meaning from it, that should be observed. However, the divine intent of the sign was to describe the incarnation of Immanuel through the virgin mother. No earthly mind could have ever imagined that the eternal God could be within the womb of a woman. Perhaps this is what Jeremiah meant: ". . . for the Lord hath created a new thing in the earth, a woman shall compass a man" (Jer. 31:22).

17 The Genealogical Dilemma

Most contemporary Americans cannot give the maiden names of their great grandmothers or the vocations of their great grandfathers. They seemingly pay little interest to their family ancestry. However, it was not so with the Jew. To him, genealogies were *most* important. Among other things, the birthright, given to the firstborn son, involved a double inheritance, family leadership, vocational opportunities, and land ownership. That is why genealogies were found throughout the Old Testament. After the Babylonian exile, the lack of proof of a genealogical listing prevented some priests from performing their ministries (Neh. 7:64). Genealogical registers were so carefully maintained by families and tribes that a Jew in the first century could trace his lineage back two thousand years to the twelve sons of Jacob (cf. Luke 2:36; Phil. 3:5). These genealogical records were destroyed in A.D. 70 when the Romans ransacked Jerusalem and scattered the Palestinian Jews.

The New Testament contains two important genealogies (Matt. 1:1-17; Luke 3:23-38). It is no coincidence that they are found in the very two Gospels that relate the historical narratives of the virgin birth of Jesus Christ. In order for Christ to be acknowledged as the King of the Jews, it must be demonstrated that His physical and legal ancestry can be traced both to Abraham and to David. This is why the New Testament opens with the words: "The book of the generation of Jesus Christ, the son of David, the son of Abraham" (Matt. 1:1). Basic to the reality of the virgin birth is an understanding of the true meaning and purpose of the two genealogies.

Their accuracy has long been criticized by liberal theologians. Pike and Kennedy said that they were "inconsistent with one another." [1] In a *Life* article on the person and ministry of Jesus, Robert Coughlan boldly asserted: "On the other hand, both Gospel writers give genealogies showing that Jesus was a descendant of King David through the male line—that is, the line of Joseph—an incongruity increased still more by the fact that the genealogies differ." [2] *If* both genealogies did record Joseph's physical lineage, then Coughlan was indeed correct; however, no reputable evangelical embraces that position. Coughlan's rejection of the accuracy of the two genealogies was based upon his subjective equation of the two. He nowhere proved that they both belonged to Joseph. His simple assumption led to another typical straw man argument.

A close study of the two genealogies will reveal both similarities and differences. Both Matthew and Luke record the same names from Abraham to David. Both mention Joseph and Jesus together in the same verse (Matt. 1:16; Luke 3:23). The differences however are more numerous, and that fact should be expected if the genealogies reveal the physical descent of two different people. Matthew began his list with Abraham and progressed toward Jesus whereas Luke began with Jesus and worked backwards past Abraham all the way to Adam. Thus, Matthew went from father to son whereas Luke went from son to father. Matthew mentioned five women who were married to five key men (Tamar, Rahab, Roth, Bathsheba or "her that had been the wife of Urias," and Mary); no women were recorded by Luke. Matthew arbitrarily divided his genealogy into three sets of fourteen generations each whereas Luke gave the exhaustive listing. Although Matthew listed only forty-one names, he counted David twice. The latter appeared both at the end of the first grouping and at the start of the second series. His lists thus were: Abraham to David; David to Josiah; and Jehoiachin to Jesus. Matthew's list contained the names of the kings of Judah; Luke's genealogy included no king. A key difference is the fact that Matthew traced the physical line of David through Solomon (1:6–7) whereas Luke recorded it through another son, Nathan (3:31). Matthew used the typical genealogical literary motif of "A begat B and B begat C" whereas Luke employed "C which was the son of B which was the son of A." Another key difference can be found in those verses that relate Jesus to Joseph. Matthew wrote: "And Jacob begat Joseph the husband of Mary, of whom was born Jesus, who is called Christ" (1:16). Luke said: "And Jesus himself began to be about thirty years of age, being (as was supposed) the son of Joseph, which was the son of Heli" (3:23). Matthew did not say that Joseph begat Jesus; his omission of "begat" is most significant. However, how could Joseph be begotten of Jacob and still be the son of Heli? This problem will be solved later.

Omissions in the lists are obvious, but this practice had been done before. Six generations of Ezra's own priestly ancestry were deliberately omitted in his own book (Ezra 7:1-5 cf. 1 Chron. 6:5-15). The kingly names of Ahaziah, Joash, and Amaziah were omitted between Jehoram and Uzziah (Matt. 1:8). The relationship of Josiah to Jehoiachin was that of grandfather to grandson with the intermediary Jehoiakim omitted (Matt. 1:11). No omissions are noted in Luke. In fact, he included the name of Cainan which was not found in the Genesis listing (3:36 cf. Gen. 11:12). Walvoord candidly observed: "It should be clear that genealogies are not necessarily complete, the main point being legitimate descent rather than inclusion of all the links in the genealogy." [3] Just as Ahaziah was called the son of Jehoshaphat when he really was a grandson (2 Chron. 22:9) so Jesus could rightfully be called both the son of David and the son of Abraham. Even the angel addressed Joseph as "thou son of David" (Matt. 1:20). These relationships must be viewed from the Jewish perspective, not from that of the western hemisphere.

Matthew listed twenty-seven names that came between David and Jesus whereas Luke recorded forty-one names for the same period. All are different with three possible exceptions. Can Matthan be the same as Matthat (Matt. 1:15 cf. Luke 3:24)? In the Jehoiachin-Salathiel-Zorobabel-Abiud and the Rhesa-Zorobabel-Salathiel-Neri groupings (Matt. 1:12-13 cf. Luke 3:27), should the middle two names be equated? Quite possibly through the law of Levirate marriage they could be identified as one and the same, but it is more plausible to view them as different individuals with coincidental same names.

The genealogical lists from Adam to the close of Biblical history can be checked against the Old Testament for their authenticity; however the names of individuals who lived in the four-hundred-year intertestamental period must have been gleaned from available registers in the synagogues or in the temple. The fact that Matthew included the names of women shows that he did not copy the genealogical record name by name. Rather, he selected those names that were pertinent to his purpose and inserted his editorial comments at will.

Now that the characteristics of the genealogies have been observed, how should they be interpreted? What is the relationship of the virgin birth of Jesus Christ to them?

One position is that Matthew recorded Joseph's physical descent from Abraham and David and that Luke gave his legal lineage. This view states that Jacob (Matt. 1:15) and Heli (Luke 3:23) were brothers. Heli became married and died, leaving no children. According to the law of Levirate marriage illustrated in the Old Testament union of Ruth and Boaz (Ruth 4:1–17 cf. Deut. 25: 5–10), the nearest single relative was supposed to marry the widow. The first son born to this second marriage would carry on the legal inheritance of the dead brother. Thus, Jacob married Heli's widow, and Joseph was born to that union. In that way, he could be both the physical son of Jacob and the legal son of Heli. This view is further strengthened if Matthan and Matthat are equated (Matt. 1:15 cf. Luke 3:24). However, there are some real problems with this view. Why are the grandfathers of Jacob and Heli different? Why do the two lines go back to two different sons of David?

A second position reverses the order of the first. It states that Matthew gave the legal lineage of Joseph whereas Luke recorded his physical background. Machen, who accepted this view, argued that the verb "begat" did not connote physical generation, but rather the legal designation of the heir apparent.[4] However, this is a movement away from the natural usage of "begat." Although direct father-son relationships were not always indicated by "begat" (Matt. 1:8, 11), a physical descent was certainly involved.

It is best, though, to conclude that Matthew recorded the physical descent of Joseph and that Luke listed the physical ancestry

of Mary. This view protects the ordinary usage of "begat."
Thus, Jacob was the real father of Joseph. Although a poor
carpenter, Joseph was still a member of the royal family of
David, both physically and legally. This is why the angel addressed him as "thou son of David" (Matt. 1:20). Joseph was
prominent in Matthew's narrative: the angel explained Mary's
pregnancy to *him* (1:18–25), warned *him* to take Mary and
Jesus into Egypt to avoid the wrath of Herod's decree (2:13–15),
informed *him* about the death of Herod (2:19–21), and God admonished *him* to go to Nazareth (2:22).

On the other hand, Luke approached the birth of Jesus from
Mary's viewpoint: Gabriel announced to *her* the details of the
virgin birth and of the incarnation (1:26–38); *she* went to the
house of Elisabeth and was praised by the latter (1:39–45);
she uttered her magnificat (1:46–56); *she* delivered her baby
(2:1–7); *she* pondered the sayings of the shepherds (2:8–20);
a purification sacrifice was offered for *her* (2:21–24); Simeon addressed himself to *her* (2:34–35); and *she* spoke to the twelve-
year-old Jesus in the temple (2:48). Heli then was the father of
Mary, the father-in-law of Joseph, and the physical and legal
grandfather of Jesus. The critical phrase "being (as was supposed)
the son of Joseph which was the son of Heli, which was the son
of Matthat, which was the son of Levi" (Luke 3:23–24 has a
critical Greek construction: *on huios hos enomizeto Joseph tou
Eli tou Matthat tou Levi*. The word *tou* is the Greek article "the."
It occurs before every proper name in the long sequence, *except
one*: Joseph! The word "son" *(huios)* occurs only once, but is
implied throughout the sequence by the genitive article of relationship. The translators of the Authorized Version recognized
these two grammatical phenomena. Outside of the first reference,
they put the words "the son" into italics. They also put the phrase
"as was supposed" into a parenthesis, but here they erred. No
parenthesis marks occurred in the original Greek text. Therefore,
their placement of the parenthesis marks was arbitrary. Because
of the words "as was supposed," no linguist doubts that a parenthesis was intended. But, what words should be incorporated
within the parenthesis? Since the article *tou* does not appear before Joseph, it should be clear that he was to be included. The

text thus should read: "being the son (as was supposed of Joseph) of Heli, the son of Matthat, the son of Levi." Since women did not appear in direct genealogical listings, Joseph stood in Mary's place, but Luke was careful to note that there was no physical connection between Joseph and either Jesus or Heli.

In order for Jesus Christ to be the rightful king of the Jews, he had to be both the physical and the legal son of Abraham and of David, thus making Him the heir to all of the Abrahamic and Davidic covenant promises. How do the genealogies demonstrate this?

Robert T. Ketcham, the past national representative of the General Association of Regular Baptist Churches, claimed that both the legal and the physical rights came to Jesus through His mother, Mary.[5] Mary was definitely of the house of David (Luke 1:27). Machen argued that this particular phrase referred to Joseph, but why would Luke later identify Joseph as "of the house and lineage of David" (2:4) if he had already done it before? Ketcham's view maintained that Heli had no sons and only one daughter, Mary. According to the law of inheritance for a "daughters only" family, a daughter had to marry within her own tribe in order to keep the inheritance (Num. 27:1–11 cf. 36:1–13). Thus, Mary in order to pass on to her physical son the legal inheritance of the family of David had to marry a man within the tribe of Judah. Thus, Matthew traced Joseph's physical ancestry back to David and to Judah to demonstrate that Mary had followed the proper procedure. This view must be regarded as a very plausible option.

In the author's opinion, however, the best position is that Jesus received His physical right to the throne of David through Mary and His legal right from Joseph. In an excellent volume *Jesus' Title to the Throne of David,* W. W. Barndollar, a retired professor at the Baptist Bible College of Pennsylvania, demonstrated conclusively that the promises of the Davidic covenant and the legal right to rule as Israel's king passed as the birthright from David to Solomon and to and through the remaining ruling kings of Judah. There is no indication in Scripture that the legal right stopped at Jehoiachin (597 B.C.), reverted back to David, and then was reinstituted through the line of Nathan, another son of

David and a physical ancestor of Mary. In David's charge to
Solomon to build the temple, David reiterated these words from
God:

> Behold, a son shall be born to thee, who shall be a man of rest; and
> I will give him rest from all his enemies round about: for his name
> shall be Solomon, and I will give peace and quietness unto Israel in
> his days.
> He shall build an house for my name; and he shall be my son, and
> I will be his father; and I will establish the throne of his kingdom over
> Israel for ever (1 Chron. 22:9–10).

God told David earlier: "And thine house and thy kingdom shall
be established for ever before thee: thy throne shall be established
for ever" (2 Sam. 7:16). The word "for ever" means the same for
Solomon as it did for David. Even Adonijah, the usurper, knew
that God planned to give the kingdom to Solomon (1 Kings
2:15). Thus, the legal right to rule as Israel's king was resident
in Joseph in the first century; however, he was prevented from
ruling for two basic reasons. Practically, the Romans controlled
Palestine and had their puppet, Herod the Great, an Idumean
and a descendant of Esau, on the throne. Among the Jewish
people, the royal family was in disrepute because the former
looked to the priests, the descendants of the Maccabean-Has-
monean priestly dynasty, for leadership. Providentially, Joseph
could not have ruled because there was a divine curse upon
him and all other physical descendants of Jehoiachin (the "Jec-
honias" of Matt. 1:11).

The following chart shows the last five kings of Judah:

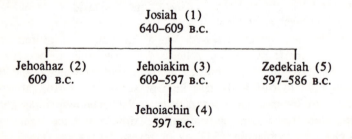

Three generations were involved in the last fifty-four years before the ultimate destruction by Babylon (586 B.C.). Three separate sons of Josiah ruled at various intervals. As far as generation sequence is concerned, Jehoiachin was closer to Joseph and Jesus than his uncle Zedekiah who was the last king. This is why the curse was placed upon Jehoiachin even though he ruled only three months in 597 B.C. The curse (Jer. 22:24–30) ended with these two stirring verses: "O earth, earth, earth, hear the word of the Lord. Thus saith the Lord, Write ye this man childless, a man that shall not prosper in his days: for no man of his seed shall prosper, sitting upon the throne of David, and ruling any more in Judah." Jehoiachin had children and grandchildren (1 Chron. 3:17–24) so the word "childless" does not apply to sterility. When Jehoiachin was taken into captivity, his successor was not his son but rather his uncle. The curse thus applied to the occupancy of the throne, not to the lack of children or the loss of the legal right to rule. Jehoiachin's descendants had the royal birthright, but they were prevented from exercising that legal right because a divine curse was upon the physical line. Earlier God had said to Jehoiakim, the father of Jehoiachin: "He shall have none to sit upon the throne of David" (Jer. 36:30). Jehoiachin, however, did sit on the throne but only for three months. The Hebrew meaning of "to sit" was "to sit firmly, continuously." This, of course, Jehoiachin did not do, and neither could his physical seed expect to reign long even if they were given that opportunity. Those who believe that the birthright reverted back many generations to David and continued again through Nathan have failed to examine thoroughly the laws of inheritance (Num. 27:8–11). Such reversion was a very slow process, going from son to daughter to brother to uncle to the next of kin. It is highly unlikely that the legal right invested in Jehoiachin would have needed to return to David in order to be continued. Actually though, there was no withdrawal of the legal right in the curse. This is what created the dilemma for Israel! How could Israel ever have a king when the legal right was passed on from one male to another who had a curse upon them that prevented them from ruling?

This is why the virgin birth of Jesus Christ was absolutely necessary.

Abraham	Adam
David	Abraham
Solomon	David
Jehoiachin	Nathan
Jacob	Heli
Joseph	Mary

└────────────────── JESUS ──────────────────┘

Physically, Jesus was the son of Adam, the son of Abraham, and the son of David through Nathan; He received this physical heritage or right through Mary. Since Joseph and Mary were legally betrothed and subsequently physically united in marriage, Jesus was recognized as the legal, firstborn son of Joseph. When Joseph named the child as bidden by the angel, he was claiming publicly the legal paternity of Jesus (Matt. 1:21, 25). Thus, the birthright which contained the legal right to rule (transmitted from David to Solomon to Jehoiachin and to Joseph) was given to Christ. The only way for Israel to have a rightful king apart from the divine curse was through the virgin birth. In this method, Jesus could receive the legal right but avoid the physical curse because he was a physical descendant of David in Nathan's line. If Jesus had been fathered by Joseph, then the curse would have kept Him from His kingship. If He had been fathered by an unknown man, then He would have been an illegitimate son, and "a bastard shall not enter into the congregation of the Lord" (Deut. 23:2).

What makes the physical descent of Jesus from Adam even more remarkable is the fact that there had to be an unbroken line of male succession. This is no small feat. Lines are easily broken by male sterility, the barrenness of the wife, the births of daughters only, the unmarried state of some men, and the early deaths of boys or young men before marriage. For example, the Abraham Lincoln family experienced only three generations of direct male succession. Abraham (1809–1865) was the father of four sons: Robert Todd (1843–1926), Edward Baker (1846–1850), William Wallace (1850–1862), and Thomas (1853–1871). The last three died respectively in infancy, youth, and early manhood before marriage. Robert Todd married and had three children: Mary, Jessie Harlan, and Abraham. Abraham (1873–1890) died before marriage. Other families can bear witness to the same difficulty in continuing the family name. However, the hand of God can be seen providentially preserving the male line all the way from Adam to Heli. The end came in Mary who conceived apart from male fertilization. The virgin birth was the miraculous end to a supernatural operation in the lives of countless thousands.

18 The Onslaughts of False Teaching

"Yea, hath God said . . . ?" (Gen. 3:1). Ever since Satan asked that question in the Garden of Eden, the authority and the authenticity of God's word, both oral and written, have been under attack. No generation has escaped the onslaught. The false prophets of Israel have been transformed into the false teachers of the church. The apostles predicted their rise. Paul wrote: "Now the Spirit speaketh expressly that in the latter times some shall depart from the faith, giving heed to seducing spirits, and doctrines of devils; speaking lies in hypocrisy; having their conscience seared with a hot iron" (1 Tim. 4:1–2). He later warned that "evil men and seducers shall wax worse and worse, deceiving, and being deceived" (2 Tim. 3:13). Such men have an outward form of godliness, but no inner spiritual power, "ever learning, and never able to come to the knowledge of the truth" (2 Tim. 3:5, 7). Peter cautioned: "But there were false prophets also among the people, even as there shall be false teachers among you, who privily shall bring in damnable heresies, even denying the Lord that bought them, and bring upon themselves swift destruction" (2 Peter 2:1). Denial of the truth takes many forms from outright repudiation to a subtle silence. Heresy can often be determined by what is not said as well as by what is spoken. The strategy of Satan includes the quiet infiltration of the ranks in addition to open warfare. Jude warned: "For there are certain men crept in unawares, who were before of old ordained to this condemnation, ungodly men, turning the grace of our God into lasciviousness, and denying the only Lord God, and our Lord Jesus Christ" (Jude 4).

In the face of such attacks, the Christian should not run away nor hide his head in the proverbial sand. The problem will not go away just because he tries to ignore it. The issue must be faced. Jude told his readers to "earnestly contend for the faith which was once delivered unto the saints" (Jude 3). After warning about anti-Christian deception, the apostle of love, John, advised: "Look to yourselves, that we lose not those things which we have wrought, but that we receive a full reward" (2 John 8). He followed with this somber warning:

Whosoever transgresseth, and abideth not in the doctrine of Christ, hath not God. He that abideth in the doctrine of Christ, he hath both the Father and the Son.
If there come any unto you, and bring not this doctrine, receive him not into your house, neither bid him God speed.
For he that biddeth him God speed is partaker of his evil deeds (2 John 9–11).

The question of Christ's deity and His virgin birth are not mere academic matters, but eternal life and death issues. The Christian should not be so naive and gullible as to believe that every "Christian" minister is fully committed to the inspiration of the Scriptures, the trinity, the deity of Christ, and His virgin birth, substitutionary atonement on the cross, and bodily resurrection. Believers should "believe not every spirit, but try the spirits whether they are of God: because many false prophets are gone out into the world" (1 John 4:1). No doubt the Ephesian elders were shocked when Paul admonished them:

For I know this, that after my departing shall grievous wolves enter in among you, not sparing the flock.
Also of your own selves shall men arise, speaking perverse things to draw away disciples after them.
Therefore watch, and remember, that by the space of three years I ceased not to warn every one night and day with tears (Acts 20:29–31).

It is one thing to expect attacks from without, but who would guess that false teachers would emerge from the very membership of the Ephesian church? The situation has not changed. Criticism is bound to come from the likes of Madalyn Murray O'Hair, but the worst attacks come from within Christendom by men who are bishops and seminary professors. These men must be identified and their denials examined. The axiom "To be forewarned is to be forearmed" is still appropriate. The author concurs with Paul's first line of defense: "And now, brethren, I commend you to God, and to the word of his grace, which is able to build you up, and to give you an inheritance among all them which are sanctified" (Acts 20:32). The second line is to know the enemy:

> For such are false apostles, deceitful workers, transforming themselves into the apostles of Christ.
> And no marvel; for Satan himself is transformed into an angel of light.
> Therefore it is no great thing if his ministers also be transformed as the ministers of righteousness; whose end shall be according to their works (2 Cor. 11:13–15).

False Concepts of Christ's Person

It is possible for ministers to preach *another* Jesus, a Jesus not proclaimed by Paul or the others (2 Cor. 11:4). Clarence Macartney claimed that a non-virgin-born Jesus would actually be a "damaged Christ." Through the years the pendulum has swung back and forth from a denial of Christ's humanity to that of His deity. In between, it has revealed a misunderstanding over the relationship of the two natures to each other in the single person of Christ. In all cases, however, a wrong view of the person of Christ has led to a logical rejection of the historicity of the virgin birth.

The early centuries saw the rise and the suppression of several heretical groups. The Docetists claimed that Jesus Christ did not possess a real human nature including a material body but that He only appeared to have human flesh. The Apollianarians stated that Jesus had a human body and soul, but no spirit. They claimed that His divine spirit took the place of the human spirit; thus Christ's humanity was incomplete. The Eutychians argued that the properties of the two natures combined to form a third type, a theanthropic nature. The Nestorians divided the person of Christ into two. The Cerinthians claimed that the spirit of the divine Christ descended upon and indwelt the natural-born Jesus at the latter's baptism and that it departed at the crucifixion. To them, the man Jesus was chosen by God for a special mission and was adopted as the Son of God at His baptism.

The Arians, ancient forerunners of the contemporary Jehovah's Witnesses, claimed that Christ was the highest creature of God's created order and that He was *like* God, but not the same as God. The famous *iota* controversy developed over the difference between *homoiousios* ("likeness") and *homoousios* ("sameness"). One Greek letter, the *iota* (English "i"), not only changed the spelling of the word, but also formed the bridge between orthodoxy and heresy. The Witnesses claim that Christ was orginally a spirit creature, Michael. Born into the world, He became a perfect human being, the equal of Adam before the fall into sin. At His death, His human nature, being sacrificed, was annihilated. As a reward for His obedience, God gave Him a divine, spirit nature. To them, there was a change of nature when an angel became a man. The angel did not acquire a second nature; thus on earth, he was only a man. There was no hypostatic union of the angelic and the human natures. There is an obvious, theological discontinuity here between the preexistent spirit state, the earthly man Jesus, and the present spirit existence.

Alva Huffer, a theologian of the Church of God General Conference (Oregon, Illinois), strangely embraced the virgin birth of Jesus, but denied His deity. He admitted that Jesus was called God, but that the title ascribed to Him was used in a secondary sense to indicate a representative of God.[1] He affirmed: "Jesus as Mediator between God and men cannot be God Himself; a mediator must be a third party."[2] Huffer did not consistently follow through with his logic. If He can't be God on that basis, then neither could He be man, and yet Huffer acknowledged His humanity. His presupposition was based upon a denial of the trinity and upon the expressions of Christ's human nature (prayer, death) being seen as a contradiction of real deity. There was no scriptural understanding of the hypostatic union of the two natures within Christ. Thus, Huffer paradoxically accepted the virgin birth without the incarnation.

In open conflict with Jesus, the religious leaders implied that He was the offspring of an illicit love affair: "We be not born of

fornication [as you may have been]" (John 8:41). After Christ
declared that they were of their father, the devil, they replied:
"Say we not well that thou art a Samaritan, and hast a devil [or
demon]" (John 8:48). Why would they say that Jesus was a
Samaritan if they knew that Joseph and Mary were His real
parents? Since Jesus never claimed openly that Joseph was His
father, they may have inferred that Joseph was not His paternal
father. Since Christ had been received joyfully by the Samaritans
(John 4:1–43), they may have reasoned that Mary had had an
affair with a Samaritan. Since He had been gracious to the woman
taken in adultery (John 8:1–11), they may have concluded that
He was being loyal to His own physical heritage. The innuendo
of illegitimacy can be detected in their dialogues with Jesus.

Nazareth was located on the main highway between Jerusalem
and the Phoenician cities of Sidon and Tyre. Full of Roman
soldiers and Greek merchants, it was notorious for its vice and
corruption. Nathanael's comment was typical of Jewish thinking:
"Can there any good thing come out of Nazareth?" (John 1:46).
The reputation of the place was soon applied to its people. Out
of this background developed the Pandera tradition. Origen in
his *Against Celsus* had to refute the charge that Jesus resulted
from a union between Mary and a soldier named Pandera or
Panthera, a concept found later in both sixth and eleventh century Jewish writings. In another form of the tradition, Joseph
Pandera was married to Mary; a neighbor Jochanan was the
seducer:

What follows occurred in the month Nisan at the end of the Feast
of the Passover at midnight. Joseph had departed at this early hour
to his school. What did this miscreant do? He arose betimes and when
Joseph had departed, the rascal entered the house and found Maria
lying apart from her husband since it was the time of her period.[3]

In the darkness, Mary thought that the intruder was Joseph
and scolded him for his actions. She conceived. When Joseph
became aware of the pregnancy, he stayed with the family until
the child was born and then deserted it. Although confused by
his departure, Mary always thought that Joseph was the real
father. This view totally disregards the Gospel narratives, reduces

Jesus to an illegitimate status, and prevents Him from having kingly rights (Deut. 23:2). Why would Zacharias and Elisabeth, righteous and blameless individuals, rejoice over Mary's child if it had been so immorally conceived (Luke 1:6, 39–45, 67–79)?

More recently, Nels Ferre, in his notorious volume *The Christian Understanding of God*, claimed that if Jesus was not the natural son of Joseph, then he had to be the illegitimate child of a German soldier. Germans were often utilized by the Romans as mercenaries; therefore Ferre speculated that they could have been stationed at the Nazareth military camp. According to him, Jesus may have resulted from a union between Mary and one of these German mercenaries. Such charges are grossly unfair and blasphemous.

Society, both secular and sacred, has generally agreed with the opening words of Mary Magdalene's song: "He's a man he's just a man." The rock opera *Jesus Christ Superstar* which contains her song, "I Don't Know How to Love Him," is based on the premise that Jesus was only human. Wonderful words have been penned about the human Jesus, but those same words convey either a silence about His deity or a denial of it. In the nineteenth century, Schleiermacher praised Jesus for His unique God-consciousness. Ritschl saw Jesus as the ideal of humanity. Through Him, men were "brought into contact with a power which is able to raise them above the iron law of necessity into the freedom and joy of the kingdom of God. Hence, to the church, *Christ has the value of God*. For God, as he is known in religion, means just this practical power to help and to deliver" [italics mine.] [4] To Ritschl, Christ's deity was pragmatic, not essential. William Adams Brown, a professor of systematic theology at Union Theological Seminary, identified Jesus both as the ideal man and the incarnate God, but this is what he meant: "It [Christ's deity] is not the declaration that God is to be found only in Jesus, but that he is everywhere and always like Jesus." [5] He claimed that the perfect man, Jesus, had both an untroubled communion with God and a self-forgetting love of man. But how could such a natural-born person exist? The Biblical doctrines of man and sin (Rom. 3:9–23; Eph. 2:1–3) prohibit such development unless that person himself had been regenerated. Was Christ the Savior because He Himself was saved and exemplary in His subsequent spirituality? The old liberal approach of Brown can still be seen in the contemporary *The Case For Theology in Liberal Perspective* by Harold De Wolf: "So clearly did he [Jesus] stand between *other men* and God and so truly did his very person indicate the *likeness and direction of God*" [italics mine].[6] To De Wolf, God was dynamically present in power wherever Christ spoke and acted.

In *Honest to God,* the radical Bishop Robinson asserted that Christ was not the most God-like man who ever lived. Rather, he agreed with the famous Dietrich Bonhoeffer: "Jesus is 'the man for others,' the one in whom Love has completely taken over, the one who is utterly open to, and united with, the ground of his being." [7] He claimed that in Jesus "here was a window into God at work." [8] In Robinson, the term "God" has been depersonalized into the concept of love. Since Christ was love in action, men can see in Him what they should be. Concerning the virgin birth, Robinson advised: "If it helps, as it has helped millions, to see in Jesus God at work, well and good. But if it merely succeeds in convincing you that he was not "one of us," then it's much better that you shouldn't believe it—for that was never its intention. I'd rather you suspended judgment than let it become a stumbling block." [9] The Jesus that Robinson believes in was not God incarnate; the Jesus that he preaches about was not virgin born. In fact, according to him, it is better not to believe in His virgin birth.

In his stormy bestseller *The Passover Plot,* Hugh Schonfield, a Jewish scholar, claimed that Jesus was the natural-born son of Joseph and Mary. He asserted: "The only way in which we can hope to know the real Jesus is by first becoming conscious of him as a man of his own time, country and people, which necessitates an intimate acquaintance with all three." [10] Schonfield saw Jesus as a master conspirator, one who believed that he was living in messianic times, who thought that he could be the messiah, and who plotted to fulfill the messianic phophecies, even those concerning his death. Lest he deemphasized the model of Jesus too much, he admitted: "Such a man could have *his godlike moments,* but could never be consistently a reflection of the Divine except for those whose notion of deity would permit the gods to share our human frailties" [italics mine].[11] One purpose behind the writing of his book was to remove the charge of deicide from the Jewish race.

It is impossible to equate a natural-born Jesus with God. The incarnation and the virgin birth cannot be separated. Mascall, a professor of historical theology at the University of London, correctly observed:

> For the Incarnation to have taken place through an ordinary act of human intercourse would in fact have involved a greater interference with the normal working of nature than for it to have taken place by a virginal conception; for in the former case there would have been the whole causal framework which normally issues in the production of a new personal subject, and God would have had to withhold his concurrence at the last moment, as it were, in order to prevent these causes from having their natural and normal effect.[12]

All wrong concepts of the person of Jesus Christ stem from a denial of His eternal deity and of His virgin birth entrance into our time-space universe.

Errors in the Gospels

Those who deny the virgin birth question the authenticity of the birth narratives and the literary and theological integrity of the writers. They do not believe that the Bible is the inspired, inerrant Word of God. Since the advent of German rationalism in the eighteenth century, the historical-critical liberal scholars have attempted to question everything within the Scriptures. Nothing is sacred to them. The *Life* writer Coughlan boldly stated: "In view of the discordance in the Nativity and Resurrection stories, one might justifiably question the historical truth of almost any story or quotation in the Gospels." [13] To them, contradictions abound and should be obvious to any honest investigator. For instance, commenting upon John 7:40–43, Pike and Kennedy remarked: "The obvious implication of this passage is that Jesus was *not* born in Bethlehem, but in Galilee. Yet the author of the Fourth Gospel makes no attempt to correct this impression. He apparently did not feel it was important to comment on the question one way or another." [14] They made Luke into a liar by stating that Jesus was not born in Bethlehem (cf. Luke 2:3-7). However, John recorded only what people were thinking about Christ's messiahship. Christ was raised in Galilee, but He was also born in Bethlehem. To follow their argument, John must have given silent assent to the charge that Jesus was demonic simply because he added no editorial comment (John 7:20). This is faulty reasoning and exegesis. Why is it that these critics are able to see plain errors in the narratives almost two thousand years after the authors originally wrote the records? Why didn't one Gospel writer change his account to harmonize with an existing Gospel? Why didn't the Church recognize these errors and correct them immediately? There are theological scholars today, banded together in the Evangelical Theological Society, who are firmly committed to the position that the Scriptures in the original writings were free from any type of error. Holding at least an earned master's degree, they teach and preach throughout the country in seminaries and colleges, both secular and Christian. Too often people have the idea that all scholars are critical of the Biblical text; this is absolutely not true. However, many liberals can be charged with bibliographic bigotry because of their refusal to read evangelical publications. What they have called contradictions have been adequately harmonized by a careful study of the text.

Honest liberals, like De Wolf,[15] admit that the Gospels teach the virgin birth of Jesus even though they deny its reality. According to Coughlan, however, they are not "histories of Jesus, but only histories of beliefs about Jesus."[16] They see the Gospels as products of the faith and life of the early church rather than authentic sources for the study of the life of Jesus. They claim that the Gospel authors wrote about the Christ of their faith rather than the real Jesus of history. This is why liberals have gone on a quest to find the historical Jesus. To them, the Jesus of history is not the same Jesus as portrayed in the Gospels. How do they expect to find Him? They prefer to study extrabiblical literature (e.g., Dead Sea Scrolls) in order to shape a personality that was conditioned by the culture of His day. The quest began with the writing of *The Aims of Jesus and His Disciples* by Hermann Reimarus in 1768. Developed later by David Strauss's *Life of Jesus* (1835), it reached a climax with the publication of Albert

Schweitzer's famous work, *The Quest of the Historical Jesus* (1906). The latter missionary doctor wrote: "Jesus as a concrete historical personality remains a stranger to our time." [17] To him, there was not enough profane historical data to make a firm judgment about Jesus' identity. He did not deny that Jesus existed, but he didn't know anything specific about Him. The reason for Schweitzer's dilemma was his adamant refusal to accept the historical trustworthiness of the Gospels. The two world wars saw the rise of existential theology, the end of the quest for a historical Jesus, and an emphasis upon the Christ of faith completely divorced from history. To the existentialist, it didn't matter whether Jesus rose bodily from a tomb. He was preoccupied with the concept that the spirit of Christ was alive in the world and in the lives of men. Historical facts became spiritually interpreted. The discovery of the Dead Sea Scrolls (1947) has awakened, however, a new quest for the historical Jesus. Since archaeological findings have supported the historical accuracy of the Gospels, more serious consideration, no doubt, will be given to those records by the new investigators.

Early critics even questioned whether the birth narratives in Matthew and Luke were part of the original Gospel writings. They suggested that they were added to the record at a later time. However, such liberals as the theologian Adolf von Harmack and the historian Edward Meyer denied this speculation. Machen ably defended the integrity of the two accounts in his classic work *The Virgin Birth of Christ*. The only records that we have of His birth are found in the two gospels. All extant Greek manuscripts of them contain these critical narratives. Critics have emphasized the apparent discrepancies in the accounts, but these can be easily reconciled. However, the similarities must not go unnoticed: birth in the days of Herod the Great (Matt. 2:1 cf. Luke 1:5); conception by the Spirit (1:18, 20 cf. 1:35); virginity of Mary (1:18, 20, 23 cf. 1:35); betrothal of Joseph and Mary (1:18 cf. 1:27; 2:5); Joseph's Davidic lineage (1:16, 20 cf. 2:4); Bethlehem as the birthplace (2:1 cf. 2:4, 6); called Jesus by angelic direction (1:21 cf. 1:31); called Savior (1:21 cf. 2:11); and residency at Nazareth (2:23 cf. 2:39).

The Bible is no ordinary book. It is redemptive history, with an equal emphasis on both words. Sproul commented: "To tell a story one believes in order to convince or persuade others of its truth does not disqualify the narrator as a credible witness. Biased observers are capable of reporting an event accurately." [18] The Gospel writers were both committed Christians and accurate historians. They did not separate the Christ of their faith from the Jesus of history. To them, those concepts referred to the same person. The Gospels must be accepted as trustworthy documents. They are "innocent until proven guilty" by real, objective evidence, not by liberal presupposition.

Myth, not Fact

In the opening song of *Jesus Christ Superstar,* Judas Iscariot reflects on stripping away "the myth from the man" and seeing Jesus as human. This is the liberal point of view.

Critical liberal theologians believe that it is their task to strip away the myth from the man. All that is supernatural is regarded as myth: virgin birth, miracles, bodily resurrection, and ascension. Speaking of the Gospels, Ernest Renan said: "They are neither biographies . . . nor fictitious legends . . . ; they are legendary biographies . . . in which historical truth and the desire to present models of virtue are combined in various degrees." [19] Robert Spivey, Associate Professor of Religion at Florida State University, and D. Moody Smith, Associate Professor of New Testament Interpretation at Duke University, claimed that the opening chapters of Matthew were largely legendary even though they admitted that the Gospel author explicitly talked about the virgin birth.[20] Schonfield bluntly stated: "There was nothing peculiar about the birth of Jesus. He was not God incarnate and no Virgin Mother bore him. The Church in its ancient zeal fathered a myth and became bound to it as dogma." [21] The difficulty in understanding modern liberal jargon is partly due to its double-talk. Boslooper recently wrote: "Both Roman Catholics and Protestants have been wrong in insisting on the literal historicity of the narratives. The virgin birth is 'myth,' in the highest and best sense of the word. Both Roman Catholics and Protestants have been correct in insisting on the importance of the virgin birth. The story of Jesus' origin proclaims a vital and provocative universal message." [22] Wrong, yet correct! Myth, yet important! These are strange words. It sounds as though blessing and cursing are coming out of the same mouth (cf. James 3:10).

Bishop Robinson believed that the language of the Bible had to be transposed into contemporary terms. Influenced by the thinking of Paul Tillich, Dietrich Bonhoeffer, and Rudolf Bultmann, he stated: "In order to express the 'trans-historical' character of the historical event of Jesus of Nazareth, the New Testament writers used the 'mythological' language of pre-existence, incarnation, ascent and descent, miraculous intervention, cosmic catastrophe, and so on." [23] Boslooper wrote that the spiritual concepts of the birth narratives "were expressed in mythical form, since it was only in this form that primitive peoples could grasp these truths, believe them, and have religious, ethical, moral, and social behavior motivated in their lives." [24] According to these men, the citizens of the first century were conditioned to think about gods becoming flesh, virgin births, and angelic visitations; thus, the Biblical authors used that literary motif in which to communicate spiritual ideas. Today, men must crack the shell of the myth to recapture the kernel of truth within. The truth should then be expressed in terms different from those of Biblical times.

According to those who demythologize the Scriptures, there is no historical factuality to the virgin birth. In fact, Boslooper charged that the fundamentalist who associates the deity of Christ with His virgin birth has actually "destroyed the Biblical, orthodox significance of the virgin birth. The total result has been that Christ has been made to be irrelevant both in his person and in his redemptive power to multitudes in modern society." [25] Soltau in his volume *The Birth of Jesus Christ* claimed that the evangelical who accepts the reality of the virgin birth "wittingly constitutes himself a sharer in a sin against the Holy Spirit of the true Gospel as transmitted to us by the Apostles." [26] R. J. Campbell, in his *The New Theology*, confessed: "I used to take the position that acceptance or non-acceptance of the doctrine of the Virgin Birth was immaterial because Christianity was quite independent of it; but later reflection has convinced me that in point of fact it operates as a hindrance to spiritual religion and a real living faith in Jesus." [27]

Thus, the fundamentalist's acceptance of the literalness of the virgin birth is termed a destruction of truth, a sin, and a hindrance. These men are aggressive, not passive, in their denial. Schonfield sarcastically asserted that the birth stories take the reader out of "the world of sober reality into the world of fairy-tale." [28] He charged that the evangelical applied to his eyes "the fairy dust called faith" in order to accept the accounts as historical.[29] Isaiah warned: "Woe unto them that call evil good, and good evil . . . Woe unto them that are wise in their own eyes, and prudent in their own sight" (Isa. 5:20–21). Schonfield called faith "fairy dust," but Hebrews stated: "Without faith it is impossible to please him" (Heb. 4:6). Paul wrote: "The just shall live by faith" (Rom. 1:17). These men have chosen reason over faith in that they have placed their confidence in their finite intellects rather than in the infallible Scriptures.

Robinson contrasted that which is real with that which is true. He claimed that the comic strip characters Andy Capp and his wife were true but not real. In them the readers see themselves. He further commented: "History records what *did* happen; myth describes what is true. Adam and Eve, Andy and Flo, are myths *because* they describe what is true." [30] He equated the literary motif of Moses with that of the cartoonist. This procedure he followed throughout his books in a denial of the reality of creation, the fall of Adam, the second coming, a post-death existence for human beings, and the virgin birth. Using his approach, men should see themselves in the experiences of the Biblical characters, but they should not affirm their existence.

According to Henry Pitney Van Dusen, a past president of the Union Theological Seminary, the spiritual meaning of the incarnation myth motif is that God can become incarnate within any man who will share the vision, purity, and purpose of God. Specifically, "in Jesus of Nazareth, God Himself was present as it is possible for him to be present in a truly human life." [31]

Bishop Robinson was completely honest when he asserted that "the non-Christian secularist view of Jesus shades imperceptibly into the estimate of his person in Liberal Christianity." [32] Evangelicals have said this for years. The Jesus of the liberal is neither the Jesus of the Gospels nor the Jesus of the fundamentalist.

These men are secular theologians who have produced a humanistic Christianity, devoid of the supernatural.

Biological Impossibility

The most popular spokesman for liberalism a generation ago, Harry Emerson Fosdick, charged that the Gospel authors phrased the account of the birth of Jesus "in terms of a biological miracle that our modern minds cannot use." [33] Since the time of David Hume, critics of biblical supernaturalism have defined a miracle as a violation of natural law. Natural law is what is observed today; therefore, since miracles, such as virgin births, do not happen in our experiences, they never did occur in the past, no matter what anyone says. They have ruled out miracles by definition! Critics have not arbitrarily picked on the virgin birth of Jesus or His walking on the water. Their problem is not with a particular miracle, but with the whole principle of miracles. They don't believe that any miracle of the Bible occurred because either they don't accept the existence of God or their God is weak or impotent. The God of the liberal is not the God of the Bible. The critic needs to repent after he reads what the angel said to Mary after his announcement of the virgin birth: "For with God nothing shall be impossible" (Luke 1:37).

A definite antisupernaturalism marks the critical approach to the biblical miracles. William Hordern, the Garrett Biblical Institute professor and former assistant to both Reinhold Niebuhr and Paul Tillich wrote: "But generally speaking, naturalism believes that the space-time universe, all of which is *in principle* knowable to science, is a self-contained unit. Therefore, satisfactory explanations can be given for all events, *in principle,* without reference to any force, power, being, or intelligence beyond the space-time universe." [34] The evangelical Christian believes in an open universe, not a closed one. He believes that prayer can be answered by God who can work in and through the activities of men to accomplish His glory and the blessing of His people. He believes that God has created the universe and that He sustains it. The natural man has termed the providential care of the universe as natural law; however, the evangelical believes that God is active, not passive, in His sustenance. Against these ordinary activities of God (e.g., gravity, water cycle), he believes that God can do extraordinary deeds. The latter can be termed as miracles. The evangelical also argues that virgin births won't occur today. This is essential to his defense of the uniqueness of Christ's birth. He is arguing for only *one* virgin birth. Boettner reasoned: "So far as ordinary events are concerned the reign of natural law is invariable. The redemption of mankind, however, is not an ordinary, but a most extraordinary event." [35] The entrance of the eternal Son of God into the created time-space universe must be seen as a unique event. The belief in the virgin birth of Jesus Christ rules out the acceptance of any other virgin birth stories. The reason is because of who He is.

Boettner correctly observed: "As a matter of fact, it is just in proportion as men lose their sense of the Divine personality of Christ that they come to doubt the reality or the necessity of the virgin birth." [36] Those who deny that Jesus was God incarnate automatically deny not only His virgin birth, but also all miracles associated with His ministry and all other miracles recorded in the Bible. Once His deity is confessed, the miracles become the reasonable thing, not the unreasonable, the credible experience, not the incredible. Even the existentialist Hordern admitted the logic of that approach.[37]

Technically, miracles have not been denied by science, but by scientism or scientific philosophy. The apologist Ramm exclaimed: "To state: 'We scientists have not discovered parthenogenesis among *homo sapiens*' is one thing; but to state: 'No virgin birth is ever possible' is bold metaphysics. It may be correct metaphysics, but the point we make is that it is not science." [38] The scientist explores what is happening now. On the basis of his findings, he can predict what will happen tomorrow or he may speculate about what happened two thousand years ago. However, he cannot prove or disprove a past historical event with present scientific inquiry. Just as the Battle of Waterloo and the reign of Julius Caesar are historical matters, so the virgin birth of Jesus Christ is a subject of historical investigation, not laboratory observation. Sproul wrote: "Though something cannot be duplicated in a controlled laboratory experiment, that does not mean that it could never have happened. No laboratory experiment can eliminate all variables, as the variable of time is always a problem. What this means simply is that the scientist can make a judgment about the probability of the virgin birth, but cannot say that it is impossible." [39] The mature scientist does not affirm the possibility or the impossibility of any phenomenon; rather, he speaks about percentages of probability.

Some have argued that if miracles occurred in the past, why don't they happen today? Miracles are nonrepeatable, extraordinary activities of God for specific purposes. They revealed the uniqueness and the power of God (Ex. 5:2 cf. 7:5); authenticated the claims of Jesus Christ (John 5:36, 10:37–38; 20:30–31), and testified to the truthfulness of the apostolic message (Matt. 10:1–8; 2 Cor. 12:12; Heb. 2:3–4). The request for viewing contemporary miracles before accepting the reality of past miracles reflects the discernment of the rich man in Hades. He asked Abraham to send the beggar Lazarus back to his five brothers to warn them about the reality of eternal judgment. Abraham refused, and stated that the brothers had access to the testimony of the Old Testament. The rich man replied: "Nay, father Abraham: but if one went unto them from the dead, they will repent" (Luke 16:30). The rich man believed that miracles would convince the unbelievers, but Abraham retorted: "If they hear not Moses and the prophets, neither will they be persuaded, though one rose from the dead" (Luke 16:31). Christ fully demonstrated the truthfulness of Abraham's remarks in His own bodily resurrection. The religious leaders, instead of repenting when they viewed the empty tomb, falsified the report that the disciples had stolen the body. Modern man is no different. If a virgin birth did occur today, scientists would not immediately believe in the virgin birth of Jesus Christ.

In *Jesus Christ Superstar*, when Christ appears before Herod Antipas during one of His trials, Herod mocks Him to produce miracles. When Christ refuses to satisfy the curiosity of Herod, the latter concludes: "You're not the Lord—you are nothing but a fraud." God does not have to prove Himself to any man. The creature doesn't make demands upon its creator. God wants men to believe in the virgin birth of Christ on the basis of His inspired, trustworthy Word.

Machen once wrote: "The New Testament without the miracles would be far easier to believe. But the trouble is, would it be worth believing?" [40] That is the point. A Christ without the virgin birth would be no Christ. Christianity would then be reduced to a mere religion, one of many to be found throughout the world. It would be man-centered rather than God-centered in its bare essence. Miracles, however, reveal God's interest in the world. They may appear impossible to finite man, but they are easily possible for an infinite, omnipotent God.

19

The Appeal
To the Pagans

In his volume *Jesus and the First Three Gospels*, Walter E. Bundy claimed: "The idea of a supernatural or virgin birth is pagan, and it must have found its way into the story of Jesus through Gentile-Christian channels." [1] In his famous sermon "Shall the Fundamentalists Win?" Fosdick asserted that in the ancient world virgin births were promoted to explain the rise of great personalities. In the *Passover Plot*, Schonfield wrote: "With the nativity stories it should have been taught by the church that they are deliberate idealizations, that intentionally they mingle the legends of the heroes of Israel and Hellas [Greece], and draw upon these legends for their basic ingredients." [2] One of the most common attacks upon the literary integrity of the Gospel writers is based upon the presupposition that they incorporated into their birth narratives the pagan concept of unusual human origin, including that of the virgin birth. Throughout the liberal denial of Christ's virgin birth, this line of argument can be found. They can't imagine how any thinking person could fail to see the parallelism between the pagan and the Christian accounts. Their readers are given the impression that it is an "open and shut" case, all in their favor.

However, this is not so. Even other liberals who do not accept the reality of the virgin birth have rejected their conclusions. The liberal *Interpreter's Bible* commented that the story of Jesus' birth was "of a very different sort" than that found in pagan mythology.[3] The *Abingdon Bible Commentary* admitted that the two birth accounts are "free from that coarseness so often characteristic of the myths and sagas that tell of the birth of great heroes from gods and goddesses." [4] An excellent refutation of the pagan derivation idea can be found in Boslooper's work *The Virgin Birth*. Although he accepted the view that the virgin birth was a myth, and not a historical reality, he repudiated any suggestion that a pagan origin contributed to his conclusion.[5] The following quotation of his evaluation of the pagan proponents is given with good reason:

Contemporary writers invariably use only secondary sources to verify such claims. The scholars whose judgment they accept rarely produced or quoted the primary sources. The literature of the old German *religiongeschichtliche Schule,* which produced this conclusion and which has become the authority for contemporary scholars who wish to perpetrate the notion that the virgin birth in the New Testament has a non-Christian source, is characterized by brief word, phrase and sentence quotations that have been lifted out of context or incorrectly translated and used to support preconceived theories. Sweeping generalizations based on questionable evidence have become dogmatic conclusions that cannot be substantiated on the basis of careful investigation.[6]

Boslooper did his work in the original sources, and they are used extensively in his book. So far, his charges have gone unrefuted by his liberal opponents. In his opinion, Boslooper stated that the basis of pagan derivation for the virgin birth literary motif had no foundation in either ancient history or literature.

There is a difference between the pagan accounts of supernatural births and the Scriptural account of the virgin birth of Jesus. A virgin birth is a supernatural birth, but a supernatural birth is not necessarily a virgin birth. The Assyrian-Babylonian stories of unusual births were based upon ancient Sumerian and Akkadian mythologies, but they contained nothing analogous to the New Testament. In a building inscription, Tukulti-Urta II (890–884 B.C.) told how the gods created him in the womb of his mother. It was claimed that the goddess of procreation superintended the conception and the womb stage of King Sennacherib (705–681 B.C.). At the conception of Buddha, his mother supposedly had this dream: "A noble elephant, white as silver or snow, having six tusks, well proportioned trunk and feet, blood-red veins, adamantine firmness of joints, and easy pace, has entered my belly." [7] Ten months later, the child was reportedly born. Hinduism claimed that the divine Vishnu, after seven reincarnations as a fish, tortoise, boar, and lion, descended into the womb of Devaki and was born as her son, the hero Krishna. In this record, deity was not only the effective agent in conception, but also the offspring. A divine factor assisted in the preservation of Zoroaster's seed, but there was a conjugal relationship between his parents.

In Graeco-Roman mythology, the mother of Perseus conceived him by Jupiter when the latter visited her in the form of a golden shower of rain. Their records reveal the births of gods and goddesses by other gods and goddesses, the birth of gods through the union of a god with a mortal woman, the birth of human heroes by the union of a god with a mortal, and the unusual births of emperors. Alexander the Great made the priests say that he was a son of Zeus. He denied that he was the son of Philip and affirmed that he was begotten by a serpent cohabiting with his mother. Later, the Roman Caesar Augustus wanted the story spread that his mother, asleep in the temple of Apollo, was visited by the god in the form of a serpent. Conceived, he was later born in the tenth month. Although this common practice revolved around ancient world leaders, no one was deceived by it. The parents of these rulers were well known. The associates accepted the claim only to flatter the proud ego of the kings.

The differences between the pagan and the Gospel accounts are so great that no one can demonstrate that the Biblical authors either borrowed from the mythological sources or refined them. Just because the pagan accounts were written first doesn't mean that the Gospel writers copied them. This is a perfect example of the logical fallacy *post hoc ergo propter hoc* ("after this, therefore, because of this"). Plato wrote about the existence of God long before Paul authored his epistles, but the latter was in no way dependent upon the Greek philosopher. The agrument of pagan derivation assumes too much in the way of parallelism and overlooks the radical differences. For example, the pagan authors did not set their stories against a legitimate historical background, whereas the Gospel narratives are inseparably connected to the historical circumstances of the first century (cf. Luke 3:1–2).

The pagan birth narratives contain records of sons born who were half god and half man. The child began to exist at his conception. However, the New Testament claimed that Jesus Christ always existed and that He acquired a human nature only in His incarnation. The result of the conception was not a diminishing or a mixture of the two natures, but a true and permanent union. Their narratives contain accounts of many supernatural births or incarnations, but the Bible emphasizes only one. Some liberals have tried to equate the birth of Jesus with the unusual circumstances surrounding the births of Isaac (Gen. 18:11), Samson (Judg. 13:2), and Samuel (1 Sam. 1:2). The mothers of all three were barren; in addition, Sarah was beyond the normal age of child bearing. God announced the birth of Isaac to Abraham and Sarah, the angel of the Lord informed the parents of Samson, and Eli told Hannah that her prayer would be answered. In spite of these strange situations, none of the women was a virgin at the time of the announcement. They conceived later after a sexual union with their husbands.

The incarnation of Christ was bathed in holiness. He was conceived in order to die redemptively for the sinful condition of men. The pagan birth stories revealed the greed and the sexual lust of the gods toward mortal women.

After the conception, Jesus experienced normal human development (Luke 2:52). In the pagan birth account of the birth of Pallas Athena who had no mother, he sprang out of the head of Zeus, full grown and in full armor. The place of Christ's birth was inconspicuous, a lowly manger in the presence of a carpenter and shepherds. The pagan accounts were recorded against a background of gross polytheism, whereas the virgin birth of Christ was written against the culture of a tenacious Jewish monotheism. The Jews never attributed a godlike origin to any of their spiritual leaders (e.g., Moses, David). Neither did the Christians elevate the apostles to that type of origin. Rather, the apostles were quick to point out their human frailties (Acts 14:11–15; Rom. 7:14–25; 1 Tim. 1:15.)

The authors traced Christ's human beginning back to the virgin birth because that is exactly what happened. Three of the four Gospels were written within thirty years of Christ's earthly life. Many who had observed His ministry were still alive at the time of their composition. No myth or legend would have been able to permeate the church in that short period of time. If the early church had recognized in the narratives of Matthew or Luke mythological influence, they would have detected and rejected it. Even the radical Harnack admitted: "The conjecture of Usener that the idea of the birth from a Virgin is a heathen myth which was received by the Christians, contradicts the entire earliest development of Christian tradition, which is free from heathen myths." [8]

Unfortunately, in their defense of the virgin birth of Christ, the early apologists argued that the heathen were the last who should reject the authenticity of Christ's birth because of their acceptance of mythological birth accounts. Justin Martyr compared it with the birth of Perseus whereas Origen appealed to the Greek idea of a cohabitation of gods with women. Origen went on to say that the pagan stories were false and that the Bible was true; however, his opponents could simply reverse the direction of his thesis. Sadly, what the church fathers gained in logic and common ground, they also lost through analogy. There were no real similarities between the conception and the incarnation of God the Son with the pagan birth stories. The former was fact; the latter was fiction.

Orr properly asked and answered this rhetorical question: "Do we as a matter of fact find, or where do we find, the idea of a divine origin of heroes or great men *taking the form of a virgin birth,* analogous to what we have in the Gospels? . . . *nowhere* in heathenism do we find this idea." [9] The concept of the virgin birth is distinctive to the New Testament interpretation of the incarnation of Jesus Christ. Other religions boasted of unusual births, but never of a genuine virgin birth used as the channel for a real incarnation. The charge of pagan derivation is absolutely false.

20 The Silence of Other Biblical Books

Another argument used by the critics is the claim that there is no mention of the virgin birth in the New Testament books ouside of Matthew and Luke. The contemporary liberal De Wolf charged that "Mark, John, and the epistles say nothing about the virgin birth." [1] Assuming that his judgment was correct, De Wolf went on to say that it was evident from the silence that the doctrine was not essential to the church's message of salvation. In a past generation, Harry Emerson Fosdick wrote: "The two men who contributed most to the church's thought of the divine meaning of the Christ were Paul and John, who never even distantly allude to the virgin birth." [2] Based upon their presupposition, the liberals have suggested a reason for this silence. J. Newton Davies, following the suggestion of Miller Burrows, [3] a professor at Yale Divinity School, conjectured: "Perhaps it is because of the difficulty of reconciling the idea of pre-existence and that of a virgin birth that John and Paul have left out of their writings all reference to the latter." [4] According to them, the concept of birth implies the creation of a new person; thus, how could a preexistent person be born? However, there is a startling admission here. These liberals are conceding that the rest of the New Testament ascribed preexistence or eternity to the person of Jesus Christ. Some evangelicals apparently have seen some truth in the liberals' position. In a special booklet printed for the conservative *Christianity Today*, Johannes Schneider admitted: "Other than this [Matthew and Luke], the New Testament says nothing about the miraculous birth of Jesus." [5] However, should such a concession be made by the evangelical? Is the rest of the New Testament silent about Christ's entrance into the world through the virgin birth? The answer is definitely negative.

The great Anglican theologian, W. H. Griffith-Thomas, in his work "The Virgin Birth—Reasons for Belief," wrote: "The preaching of the fact of the incarnation rather than the mode is the true method of presenting the Gospel; first what Christ is and only then how He came to be what He is." [6] To a lost and dying world, the early Christians preached that faith in Jesus Christ, both in His person which was both divine and human and in His redemptive work of suffering and resurrection, could only save. They did not get into debate as to how one person could be both God and man at the same time. They did not attempt to solve the paradox that He could be located in heaven and still be with Christians wherever they were. William Childs Robinson, the emeritus professor of historical theology at Columbia Theological Seminary, claimed that "what is explicit in Matthew and Luke is implicit in Paul and John." [7] It is not tenable to argue from silence to disbelief or from silence to an ignorance of the doctrine. The apostles did not record everything that they taught or knew (cf. John 20:30). In fact, the so-called silence argument of the liberal can boomerang on him. Since Paul did not mention any human father for the person Jesus, does that mean that he believed that Jesus had no human father? Most regard silence as assent. If Paul and the others did not believe in the virgin birth, should they not have corrected the earlier birth narratives? The argument of silence can be used both ways. Actually, no confession or denial should ever be based upon the argument from silence.

Actually, how many times must an event be recorded in order to have authenticity and universal acceptance by the church? The virgin birth was mentioned by two different authors at some length. Would it have been better for one man to have referred to it over one hundred times while the others gave no statement? According to Christ, "in the mouth of two or three witnesses every word may be established" (Matt. 18:16). Two witnesses are sufficient in any court of law as long as their testimonies agree and their character is unimpeachable. Only two recorded the ascension of Jesus (Mark and Luke), but both Matthew and John were there to observe it. Only Matthew mentioned the word "church" (Matt. 16:18; 18:17), but that does not mean that the others were ignorant of Jesus' prediction of the church era. None of the epistles mention Mary by name, but some of the writers

knew her personally and all believed in her existence. Why should
Luke refer to the virgin birth in the Book of Acts when he had
already demonstrated its reality to Theophilus in the Gospel? Luke
was an associate of Paul and wrote under the latter's apostolic
authority. They shared the same doctrinal convictions and
doubtless Luke learned much of his theology from Paul. Even
within Paul's thirteen epistles, one can isolate a section not
mentioned in the other books (e.g., the care of widows;
1 Tim. 5:1–16), but this does not mean that Paul failed to
instruct other individuals and churches about this type of welfare.

The charge of the liberal critic, however, must not be dodged.
Were the other writers silent on the subject of Christ's birth, or did
they refer to the event in different terminology? For example,
everyone knows that J. Paul Getty is a multimillionaire. If a
biographer records that Getty gave three million dollars to a
university and delivered a ransom of one million dollars for his
grandson, but never declares that Getty was a multimillionaire, no
one would charge the biographer of ignorance of Getty's financial
status. What he did proved who he was. So it was with the other
writers of the New Testament. They spoke to the subject of
Christ's incarnation without going into the details of the virgin
birth.

Howard Kee, a teacher at Bryn Mawr College, said that John
"gives no hint of belief in the virgin birth. Instead, he states
directly that Joseph is the father of Jesus (1:45; 6:42) and that
Jesus' birthplace was Nazareth." [8] John never declared that Joseph
was the paternal father of Jesus. The murmuring Jews
questioned: "Is not this Jesus, the son of Joseph, whose father and
mother we know? how is it then that he saith, I came down from
heaven?" (John 6:42). The Jews saw Him as a mere human and
believed that Joseph was His real physical father, but they were
mistaken. Philip's identification of Jesus as the son of Joseph
recognized the legal connection between Jesus and Joseph since
the latter was a son of David and possessed the birthright of
messianic rulership. In an earlier chapter, both the claims made
by Christ directly about Himself and the claims made for Christ
by the Biblical writers were studied. They were identical. Jesus
Christ was seen as a theanthropic person, and the only way that

He could have become human was through the virgin conception. John, though, clearly stated that the Word (Christ) who always was God "was made flesh, and dwelt among us" (John 1:1 cf. 1:14). He, divine spirit, came to be (*egeneto*) what He was not before—human. Does not this fact require a genuine incarnation without the procreation of a new person through natural generation?

A mild debate has centered about John's statement: "Which were born, not of blood, nor of the will of the flesh, nor of the will of man, but of God" (John 1:13). The majority of Greek manuscripts use the nominative, masculine, plural relative pronoun *hoi* ("who" or "which") along with the plural verb *egennethesan* ("were born"). However, a few ancient texts employed the singular personal pronoun *hos* (who) with the singular verb *egennethe* ("was born"). The plural usage would refer to those who had received Christ, who became children of God, and who were believing on His name. However, the singular usage would refer to Christ alone; thus, verse thirteen would have been a description of His virgin conception by God. The great New Testament scholar, Theodor Zahn, claimed that a triple denial of human activity was not needed to put forth the positive divine work in regeneration. In His conversation with Nicodemus, Jesus referred only to the flesh in delineating physical birth (John 3:6). Zahn concluded his study: "Tertullian was probably right in accusing the Valentinians of being the first to change the singular in verse 13 to the plural." [9] Both the patristic Irenaeus in his *Against Heresies* and Tertullian in his *On the Flesh of Christ* argued that the singular was the preferred reading. Such reputable scholars as Zahn, C. C. Torrey, and Oscar Cullmann have accepted the singular as the correct reading. Even those who accept the plural reading see a definite analogy between the new birth of the believing sinner and the virgin birth of Christ. The believer became saved not because he inherited a Christian nature from his parents ("bloods") nor because a Christian parent or friend desired this experience for him nor because he made the decision all by himself. The new birth originates with God, not with human initiative. So Jesus Christ was not the result of the union of two willing parents nor of the immoral lust of an illicit relationship nor of the will of Mary or Joseph. He was the eternal Son of God, the only begotten one. The singular reading must be seen as plausible.

Paul believed that Jesus Christ was both divine and human (cf. chapter two). He also believed that God became man, not that a mere man came to be deified. In several passages, he referred to the act of incarnation which involved a real human birth. To the Romans, he wrote: "Concerning his Son Jesus Christ our Lord, which was made of the seed of David according to the flesh" (Rom. 1:3). He was the son of God before He became the seed of David. The resurrection demonstrated that truth (1:4). He later claimed that Adam was "the figure of him [Christ] that was to come" (Rom. 5:14). Adam did not become a man by natural generation, and neither did Christ. Also, he asserted that God sent "his own Son in the likeness of sinful flesh" (Rom. 8:3). He was the Son of God before He was sent. He did not come in sinful flesh because no sin nature had been transmitted to Him. He did not come in the likeness of flesh because He had a real human nature. The likeness referred to the adjective "sinful." Everyone thought that Jesus was just another typical sinful human being, but His divine personality and virgin conception maintained His sinlessness. Again, Paul wrote: "Whose are the fathers, and of whom as concerning the flesh Christ came, who is over all, God blessed for ever" (Rom. 9:5). Paul saw Him both as divine and Jewish.

Elsewhere in his epistles, Paul stated this contrast between Adam and Jesus: "The first man is of the earth, earthy: the second man is the Lord from heaven" (1 Cor. 15:47). If Christ was the Lord from heaven, how did He become a man? Certainly this verse implies a natural birth, if not the virgin birth. To the Galatians, he penned: "But when the fulness of the time was come, God sent forth his Son, made of a woman, made under the law" (Gal. 4:4). The word "made" is the aorist participle *genomenon,* the same verb stem and tense used by John (John 1:14). Does "made of a woman" only suggest a human birth, a generation by two parents, or does it actually teach the virgin birth? It is significant that in this same chapter Paul used a different verb *gennao* to describe the births of Isaac and Ishmael (Gal. 4:23, 29). Why did Paul change the verbs if he believed that Jesus' birth was of the same type as those of the sons of Abraham? It is clear that Paul saw a significant difference between the two. Since He was sent by His heavenly Father, He had no human father, but He came to be human out of the womb of a human mother.

The incarnation is clearly taught in the famous Kenosis passage: "who [Christ], being in the form of God, thought it not robbery to be equal with God: But made himself of no reputation, and took upon him the form of a servant, and was made in the likeness of men: And being found in fashion as a man" (Phil. 2:6–8a). His preincarnate existence and deity can be seen in the phrases "being in the form of God" and "equal with God." The gaining of a human nature can be ascertained from the phrases "took upon him the form of a servant," "made in the likeness of men," and "being found in fashion as a man." Of the three phrases, the first refers to the decretive act of self-humiliation, the second to the actual incarnation, and the third to His human identification by men. The form of God involved the sovereign right to be served by others; in His condescension, He would serve others. The word "made" is *genomenos,* used elsewhere of the incarnation (John 1:14; Gal. 4:4). The incarnation involved a change of form, not content or essential being. Just as the content of a bottle can be poured into a glass without changing its nature, so the divine person of Christ was not affected when His glorious outward expression was veiled in human flesh. The liberals have completely misrepresented the evangelical concept of the kenosis. Brown wrote: "The philosophical dificulties of this theory are so obvious as to need no extended comment. . . . What manner of being is this who knows himself to be God, yet is destitute of the attributes of God." [10] More recently, Bishop Robinson stated: "Yet the fatal weakness of this theory as it is stated in supranaturalist terms is that it represents Christ as stripping himself precisely of those attributes of transcendance which make him the revelation of God. The underlying assumption is that it is his omnipotence, his omniscience, and all that makes him 'superhuman,' that must be shed in order for him to become truly man." [11] Although these two liberals lived a generation apart, their denials are identical. However, Christ did not have to give up deity in order to become man. God can never be less that what His nature requires Him to be.

To Timothy, Paul wrote: "And without controversy great is the mystery of godliness: God was manifest in the flesh" (1 Tim. 1:16). Later, he added that Christ was "of the seed of David" (2 Tim. 2:8). Some commentators have detected the virgin birth in the obscure passage: ". . . she shall be saved in childbearing" (1 Tim. 2:15). The Greek text reads *"the child-bearing."* Could this be a possible reference to the fulfillment of the prophecy given in the Garden of Eden (Gen. 3:15)? It is a plausible option.

The Book of Hebrews claims both that Jesus Christ was God (1:1–14) and that He was "made a little lower than the angels" (2:9), that He partook of flesh and blood (2:14), and that "he took on him the seed of Abraham" (2:16). Peter said that Christ "was manifest in these last times for you" (1 Peter 1:20).

The charge of the liberal that no reference to the virgin birth or incarnation can be found outside of Matthew and Luke cannot stand up under close scrutiny of the books. Although the seven other authors did not use the word "virgin," they spoke of Christ as God and affirmed His entrance into humanity. The only logical way for this incarnation to have occurred was through the virgin birth.

CONCLUSION: Why the

Doctrine Is Essential

The world has experienced unusual births. In 1934, the birth of the Dionne quintuplets received international notoriety. More recently, the United States has seen the births of the Fisher quintuplets and the spectacular Stanek sextuplets, born in Colorado in September, 1973. With the increase of the usage of fertility drugs and pills, more multiple births will doubtless be reported. However, the only unique birth still remains the virgin birth of Jesus Christ. There was none like His before nor after nor ever will be.

The great evangelist and author John R. Rice asserted: "All Christianity stands or falls with the doctrine of the virgin birth. If Jesus had a human father, then the Bible is not true." [1] To confess the virgin birth is to confess the deity of Christ; to confess the deity of Christ is to confess the virgin birth. They are inseparable, Siamese twins. Conversely, to deny the virgin birth is to deny the deity of Christ; to deny the deity of Christ is to deny the virgin birth. No person can logically accept one and reject the other. Christ is not God because He was virgin born, but because He was and is God, He had to be virgin born to obtain a real humanity.

Does that mean that a person must be informed about the virgin birth and believe in it before he can become a genuine, saved Christian? That question cannot be answered with a simple "yes" or "no" answer. In dealing with drunks, collegians, or socialites, counsellors probably never refer to the virgin birth. The latter must point out man's sinful condition, his inability to save himself, and his need to accept the redemptive provisions of Christ's death and resurrection. The invitation usually centers around the question: "Do you want to receive Jesus Christ as your personal Savior?" In essence, the evangelist is beseeching the sinner to put his trust in a person and in what that person had done. But this is the critical area. Who is this person? Faith in a mere human Jesus won't save anyone. Actually, faith in God only won't save either (James 2:19). Saving faith must rest in Him who is both divine and human. But how did He come to have two natures? The Scriptural explanation is through the virgin birth. In counselling, the evangelist must be sure that the sinner is asked to trust in Jesus Christ who was God but who also became man in order to die for the sins of men and to rise again for their justification. After the believing sinner has been regenerated, he will automatically believe the record that Christ became incarnate through the virgin birth. If he rejects the truth of the virgin birth once that it is shown to him, then that is evidence that he put his faith in a marred Jesus, one who was not God incarnate. Thus, he was not really saved in the first place.

Evangelical churches should exercise great discernment in screening pastoral candidates for their empty pulpits and in ordaining college and seminary graduates into the ministry. Special attention should be given to the Christological viewpoint. It is not enough to ask a candidate whether he believes in the virgin birth or in the incarnation. Ask him what he means by those terms. There are too many "Bishop Robinsons" around who confess that Christ was the Son of God but deny that He was God the Son. They claim that the incarnation and the creation of Adam were true but not real.

In a red-flag article in *Christianity Today* entitled "A 'New' Christology Challenges the Church," Klaas Runia, a teacher at the Seminary of the Reformed Churches of the Netherlands, warned that the doctrines of the trinity and of the hypostatic union within the person of Christ are *now* being opposed "by people who up till now were never regarded as liberals." [2] He claimed that figurative language has crept into the vocabulary of these "evangelical" theologians. Runia charged: "They do not mean that Jesus is *essentially* the Son of God; it is only by way of speaking. In himself Jesus is *man* and no more." [3] Liberal and existential thinking about the person of Christ unfortunately is being absorbed by "evangelicals" who are being trained and influenced by the liberal framework. Runia concluded: "The seriousness of the situation should not be underestimated. There are clear indications that the Christological battle of the early church has to be fought all over again." [4]

In the preface, the author pointed out the existence of shallow and fuzzy thinking about the trinity and the person of the incarnate Christ by his own students who have been raised in Christian homes and evangelical churches. It is now time to preach, to teach, and to write about the great themes of Christology. Foremost among these are the incarnation and the virgin birth, the doctrines of the deity of Jesus Christ.

NOTES

Introduction

1 John A. T. Robinson, *But That I Can't Believe!* (The New American Library, 1967) p. 31.
2 *Ibid.*, p. 32.
3 Cited by Diane Kennedy Pike and R. Scott Kennedy, *The Wilderness Revolt* (New York: Doubleday, 1972), p. 261.

Chapter 1

1 Samuel J. Mikolaski, *The Triune God* (Washington: Christianity Today, n.d.), p. 31.
2 Loraine Boettner, *Studies in Theology* (Philadelphia: The Presbyterian and Reformed Publishing Co., 1964), p. 109.
3 *Ibid.*, pp. 106–107.
4 *Ibid.*, p. 119.
5 Cited by Oswald J. Sanders, *Cults and Isms* (Grand Rapids: Zondervan, 1962), p. 81.
6 *"The Word"—Who is He? According to John* (Brooklyn: Watchtower Bible and Tract Society, 1962), p. 7.
7 J. V. Langmead Casserley, "The Virgin Birth," *A Handbook of Christian Theology* (New York: Living Age Books, 1958), p. 370.
8 Mikolaski, *op. cit.*, p. 10.

Chapter 2

1 This verse will be discussed in detail in a later chapter.
2 J. Barton Payne, *The Theology of the Older Testament* (Grand Rapids: Zondervan, 1962), p. 262.
3 F. F. Bruce, "The Person of Christ," *Christianity Today* (Oct. 13, 1961), p. 30.

Chapter 3

1 Ernest Cadman Colwell, "A Definite Rule for the Use of the Article in the Greek New Testament," *Journal of Biblical Literature*, LXX (1933), pp. 12–31.
2 Cited by H. E. Dana and Julius R. Mantey, *A Manual Grammar of the Greek New Testament* (New York: Macmillan, 1953), p. 147.

Chapter 4

1 If Jesus did not speak the content of this verse to Nicodemus, then it describes John's belief in Christ's heavenly origin.
2 Reported by the Associated Press wire service, June 23, 1969.
3 *The Jewish Encyclopedia* (New York: Funk and Wagnalls, 1906), Vol. 8, p. 511.
4 John H. Gerstner, *Reasons For Faith* (New York: Harper & Brothers, 1960), p. 104.
5 *Ibid.*, p. 105.
6 William G. T. Shedd, *Dogmatic Theology* (Grand Rapids: Zondervan, N.D.), Vol. I, p. 323.

Chapter 5

1 Cited by R. C. Sproul, *The Symbol* (Nutley: The Presbyterian and Reformed Publishing Co., 1973), p. 48.
2 Boettner, *op. cit.*, p. 152.
3 John A. T. Robinson, *Honest to God* (Philadelphia: The Westminster Press, 1963), p. 72.
4 Mikolaski, *op. cit.*, p. 12.
5 John R. Rice, *Is Jesus God?* (Murfreesboro, Tenn: Sword of the Lord, 1964), p. 71.
6 John F. Walvoord, *Jesus Christ Our Lord* (Chicago: Moody Press, 1969), p. 40.
7 Charles R. Erdman, *The Epistles of Paul to the Colossians and to Philemon* (Philadelphia: Westminster Press, n.d.), p. 47.
8 Wilbur M. Smith, *The Supernaturalness of Christ* (Boston: W. A. Wilde Co., 1944), p. 89.
9 Bernard Ramm, *Protestant Christian Evidences* (Chicago: Moody Press, 1959), pp. 163–183.

Chapter 6

1 Smith, *op. cit.*, p. 9.
2 Cited by Smith, *op. cit.*, p. 100.

Chapter 7

1 Pike and Kennedy, *op. cit.*, p. 60. The prophecy of Isaiah 7:14 will be discussed later in detail.
2 *The New Scofield Reference Bible* (New York: Oxford University Press), footnote #4, p. 992.
3 William Barclay, *The Gospel of Matthew* (Philadelphia: The Westminster Press, 1958), Vol. I, p. 10.
4 *Ibid.*, p. 13.
5 R. C. H. Lenski, *The Interpretation of Saint Matthew's Gospel* (Columbus: Wartsburg Press, 1943), p. 37.
6 Louis Matthews Sweet, "The Virgin Birth," *International Standard Bible Encyclopedia* (Grand Rapids: Wm. B. Eerdmans Publishing Co., 1952), Vol. 5, p. 3052.

Chapter 8

1 Cited by James Orr, *The Virgin Birth of Christ* (New York: Charles Scribner's Son, 1907), p. 138. Reprint by College Press, Joplin, Mo., 1972.
2 Thomas Boslooper, *The Virgin Birth* (Philadelphia: The Westminster Press, 1962), p. 27.

Chapter 9

1 A. T. Robertson, *Word Pictures in the New Testament* (Nashville: Broadman Press, 1930), Vol. I, p. 7.
2 Aloys Dirksen, *A Life of Christ* (New York: Holt, Rinehart and Winston, 1962), p. 104.

Chapter 10

1 Bolton Davidheiser, *To Be As God* (Nutley, N.J.: Presbyterian and Reformed Publishing Co., 1972), pp. 8–10.
2 Smith, *op. cit.*, p. 92.
3 Bernard Ramm, *The Christian View of Science and Scripture* (London: The Paternoster Press, 1967), p. 205.
4 Henry M. Morris, *The Bible Has The Answer* (Nutley, N.J.: The Craig Press, 1971), p. 31.

Chapter 11

1 Cited by Boslooper, *op. cit.*, p. 71.

Chapter 12

1 Robinson, *Honest to God*, p. 67.
2 L. Berkhof, *Systematic Theology* (Grand Rapids: Wm. B. Eerdmans Publishing Co., 1953), p. 322.
3 Bruce, *op. cit.*, p. 30.
4 Berkhof, *op. cit.*, p. 321.
5 *Ibid.*
6 *Ibid.*
7 *Ibid.* p. 316
8 Robinson, *Honest to God*, p. 77.
9 Hugh J. Schonfield, *The Passover Plot* (New York: Bantam Books, 1967), p. 67.
10 Berkhof, *op. cit.*, p. 322.
11 Shedd, *op. cit.*, Vol. II, p. 328.
12 *Ibid.*, p. 329.
13 Walvoord, *op. cit.*, p. 115.

Chapter 13

1 Cited by Shedd, *op. cit.*, pp. 302–303.
2 Walter R. Martin, *Essential Christianity* (Grand Rapids: Zondervan Publishing House, 1962), p. 37. footnote.
3 J. S. Whale, *Christian Doctrine* (London: Cambridge University Press, 1961), p. 99.
4 Shedd, *op. cit.*, p. 332.

5 *Ibid.*, p. 333.
6 *Ibid.*
7 Cited by Boettner, *op. cit.*, p. 211.

Chapter 14

1 Berkhof, *op. cit.*, p. 22.
2 J. Gresham Machen, *The Virgin Birth of Christ* (Grand Rapids: Baker Book House, 1967), p. 3.

Chapter 15

1 Bruce, *op. cit.*, p. 31.
2 Boettner, *op. cit.*, pp. 136–137.
3 The veil that separated the two sanctuaries of the Mosaic tabernacle was a type of His crucified flesh (Heb. 10:19–20). The rock that Moses smote in the wilderness to get water was a symbol of the smitten Christ (Ex. 17:6 cf 1 Cor. 10:4).

Chapter 16

1 Herbert M. Wolf, "A Solution to the Immanuel Prophecy in Isaiah 7:14–8:22," *Journal of Biblical Literature*, Vol. 91, No. 4 (December, 1972), p. 456.
2 Casserley, *op. cit.*, p. 369.
3 *The Jewish Encyclopedia, op. cit.*, Vol. 8, p. 506.
4 Cited by Orr, *op. cit.*, p. 125.
5 Edward E. Hindson, "Development of the Interpretation of Isaiah 7:14," *Grace Journal*, Vol. 10, No. 2 (Spring, 1969), pp. 19–25.
6 Alva J. McClain, "The Virgin Birth in the RSV," *The Brethren Missionary Herald* (February 28, 1953), p. 138.
7 G. B. Gray, *A Critical and Exegetical Commentary on the Book of Isaiah*, pp. 126–127.
8 Merrill F. Unger, *Unger's Bible Dictionary* (Chicago: Moody Press, 1957), p. 1159.
9 George L. Lawlor, *Almah . . . Virgin or Young Woman?* (Des Plaines, Ill.: Regular Baptist Press, 1973), pp. 20–22.
10 Unger, *loc. cit.*
11 Robert Dick Wilson, "The Meaning of Alma (A.V. 'virgin') in Isaiah VII. 14," *Princeton Theological Review*, Vol. 24, No. 2 (April, 1926), p. 316.
12 J. A. Alexander, *Commentary on the Prophecies of Isaiah* (Grand Rapids: Zondervan Publishing House, 1953 edition), p. 172.

Chapter 17

1 Pike and Kennedy, *op. cit.*, p. 66.
2 Robert Coughlan, "Who Was The Man Jesus?", *Life*, Vol. 57, No. 26 (December 25, 1964), p. 90.
3 John F. Walvoord, "The Incarnation of the Son of God," *Bibliotheca Sacra*, Vol. 117, No. 465 (January, 1960), p. 11.
4 Machen, *op. cit.*, p. 204.

5 Cited by Emery H. Bancroft, *Elementary Theology* (Hayward, Calif.: J. F. May Press, 1948), pp. 88–92.

Chapter 18

1 Alva G. Huffer, *Systematic Theology* (Oregon, Ill.: The Restitution Herald, 1965), p. 251.
2 *Ibid.*, p. 250.
3 Cited by Boslooper, *op. cit.*, p. 39.
4 Cited by William Adams Brown, *Christian Theology* (New York: Charles Scribner's Sons, 1907), p. 340.
5 *Ibid.*, pp. 329, 347.
6 L. Harold De Wolf, *The Case For Theology in Liberal Perspective* (Philadelphia: The Westminster Press, 1959), p. 74.
7 Robinson, *Honest to God*, p. 76.
8 *Ibid.*, p. 71.
9 Robinson, *But That I Can't Believe!*, p. 47.
10 Hugh J. Schonfield, *The Passover Plot* (New York: Bantam Books, 1967), p. 3.
11 *Ibid.*, p. 4.
12 E. L. Mascall, *Christian Theology and Natural Science* (London: Archon Books, 1965), p. 311.
13 Coughlan, *op. cit.*, p. 91.
14 Pike and Kennedy, *op. cit.*, p. 295.
15 De Wolf, *op. cit.*, pp. 60–61.
16 Coughlan, *op. cit.*, p. 100.
17 Albert Schweitzer, *My Life and Thought* (London: Allen and Univin, 1933), p. 399.
18 Sproul, *op. cit.*, p. 45.
19 Cited by Coughlan, *op. cit.*, p. 99.
20 Robert A. Spivey and D. Moody Smith, Jr., *Anatomy of the New Testament* (New York: Macmillan, 1969), pp. 98, 100.
21 Schonfield, *op. cit.*, p. 42.
22 Boslooper, *op. cit.*, p. 21.
23 Robinson, *Honest to God*, p. 24.
24 Boslooper, *op. cit.*, p. 236.
25 *Ibid.*, pp. 234–235.
26 Cited by Orr, *op. cit.*, p. 2.
27 *Ibid.*, pp. 2–3.
28 Schonfield, *op. cit.*, p. 41.
29 *Ibid.*
30 Robinson, *But That I Can't Believe!*, p. 40.
31 Cited by Wilbur M. Smith, *Therefore, Stand* (Boston: W. A. Wilde Co., 1950), p. 55.
32 Robinson, *Honest to God*, p. 68.
33 Cited by G. W. McPherson, *The Virgin Birth* (Yonkers, N.Y.: Yonkers Book Company, 1922), p. 7.
34 William Hordern, *The Case For a New Reformation Theology* (Philadelphia: The Westminster Press, 1959), p. 103.
35 Boettner, *op. cit.*, p. 212.
36 *Ibid.*, p. 215.
37 Hordern, *op. cit.*, p. 108.

38 Ramm, *Protestant Christian Evidences*, p. 49.
40 Machen, *Christianity and Liberalism*, p. 103.

Chapter 19

1 p. 11, cited by Boslooper, *op. cit.*, p. 135.
2 Schonfield, *op. cit.*, p. 42.
3 *The Interpreter's Bible* (New York: Abingdon Press, 1951), Vol 7, p. 254.
4 *The Abingdon Bible Commentary* (New York: The Abingdon Press, 1929), p. 957.
5 Boslooper, *op. cit.*, p. 136.
6 *Ibid.*, p. 135.
7 *Ibid.*, p. 139.
8 Cited by Orr, *op. cit.*, p. 154.
9 *Ibid.*, p. 165.

Chapter 20

1 De Wolf, *op. cit.*, p. 61.
2 Cited by McPherson, *op. cit.*, p. 4.
3 Millar Burrows, *An Outline of Biblical Theology* (Philadelphia: The Westminster Press, 1946), p. 101.
4 *The Abingdon Bible Commentary*, p. 957.
5 Johannes Schneider, "Jesus Christ: His Life and Ministry" (Washington: *Christianity Today*, n.d.), p. 24e.
6 Cited by Orr, *op. cit.*, p. 285.
7 William Childs Robinson, "The Virgin Birth—A Broader Base," *Christianity Today*, Vol. XVII, No. 5 (December 8, 1972), p. 6.
8 Howard Clark Kee, *Jesus in History* (New York: Harcourt, Brace and World, Inc., 1970), p. 197.
9 Cited by Orr, *op. cit.*, pp. 271–272.
10 Brown, *op. cit.*, p. 338.
11 Robinson, *Honest to God*, pp. 74–75.

Conclusion

1 Rice, *op. cit.*, p. 62.
2 Klaas Runia, "A 'New' Christology Challenges the Church," *Christianity Today*, Vol. XVIII, No. 7 (January 4, 1974), p. 5.
3 *Ibid.*, p. 6.
4 *Ibid.*, p. 8.

BIBLIOGRAPHY

Bancroft, Emery H. *Christian Theology*. Hayward, Calif: J. F. May Press, 1949.

Barclay, William. *The Gospel of Matthew*. 2 vols. Philadelphia: The Westminster Press, 1958.

Barndollar, W. W. *Jesus' Title to the Throne of David*. Findlay, Ohio: The Dunham Publishing Company, 1963.

Berkhof, L. *Systematic Theology*. Grand Rapids: Wm. B. Eerdmans Publishing Co., 1953.

Berkouwer, G. C. *The Work of Christ*. Grand Rapids: Wm. B. Eerdmans Publishing Co., 1965.

Boettner, Loraine. *Studies in Theology*. Philadelphia: The Presbyterian and Reformed Publishing Co., 1964.

Boslooper, Thomas. *The Virgin Birth*. Philadelphia: The Westminster Press, 1962.

Briggs, Charles A. "The Virgin Birth of our Lord," *American Journal of Theology*, Vol. 12 (April, 1908).

Brown, William Adams. *Christian Theology*. New York: Charles Scribner's Sons, 1907.

Bruce, F. F. "The Person of Christ," *Christianity Today*, October 13, 1961.

Burrows, Millar. *An Outline of Biblical Theology*. Philadelphia: The Westminster Press, 1946.

Casserley, J. V. Langmead. "The Virgin Birth," *A Handbook of Christian Theology*. New York: Living Age Books. 1958.

Chafer, Lewis Sperry. *Systematic Theology*. 7 vols. Dallas: Dallas Seminary Press, 1953.

Cheney, Johnston M. and Ellisen, Stanley A. *The Life of Christ in Stereo*. Portland, Oregon: Western Baptist Seminary Press, 1969.

Coughlan, Robert. "Who Was The Man Jesus?" *Life*, Vol. 57, No. 26 (December 25, 1964), pp. 86–101.

Davidheiser, Bolton. *To Be As God*. Nutley, N.J.: Presbyterian and Reformed Publishing Co., 1972.

De Wolf, L. Harold. *The Case For Theology In Liberal Perspective*. Philadelphia: The Westminster Press, 1959.

Dirksen, Aloys. *A Life of Christ*. New York: Holt, Rinehart and Winston, 1962.

Feinberg, Charles L. "The Virgin Birth in the Old Testament." *Bibliotheca Sacra*, Vol. 117, No. 468 (October, 1960).

Ferre, Nels F. S. *The Christian Understanding of God*. New York: Harper and Brothers, 1951.

Hanke, Howard A. *The Validity of the Virgin Birth*. Grand Rapids: Zondervan Publishing House, 1963.

Hindson, Edward E. "Development of the Interpretation of Isaiah 7:14," *Grace Journal*, Vol. 10, No. 2 (Spring, 1969), pp. 19–25.

Hordern, William. *The Case For a New Reformation Theology*. Philadelphia: The Westminster Press, 1959.

Huffer, Alva G. *Systematic Theology*. Oregon, Ill.: The Restitution Herald, 1965.

Humberd, R. I. *The Virgin Birth*. Flora, Ind: By the author, n.d.

Johnson, S. Lewis Jr. "The Genesis of Jesus," *Bibliotheca Sacra*, Vol. 122, No. 488 (October, 1965).

Kee, Howard Clark. *Jesus In History*. New York: Harcourt, Brace & World, Inc., 1970.

Kelly, Howard A. *A Scientific Man and the Bible*. Philadelphia: The Sunday School Times Company, 1925.

Lawlor, George L. *Almah . . . Virgin or Young Woman?* Des Plaines, Ill.: Regular Baptist Press, 1973.

Lenski, R. C. H. *The Interpretation of Saint Matthew's Gospel*. Columbus: Wartsburg Press, 1943.

McClain, Alva J., "The Virgin Birth in the RSV," *The Brethren Missionary Herald*, February 28, 1953.

McDonald, H.D. *Jesus—Human and Divine*. Grand Rapids: Zondervan Publishing House, 1968.

McDowell, Josh. *Evidence That Demands a Verdict*. Arrowhead Springs: Campus Crusade for Christ, 1972.

McIntosh, P. Douglas. "The Immanuel Prophecy of Isaiah" Unpublished master's thesis, Dallas Theological Seminary, 1971.

McPherson, G. W. *The Virgin Birth*. Yonkers, N.Y.: Yonkers Book Company, 1922.

Machen, J. Gresham. *The Virgin Birth of Christ*. Grand Rapids: Baker Book House, 1967.

Martin, Walter R. *Essential Christianity*. Grand Rapids: Zondervan Publishing House, 1962.

Mascall, E. L. *Christian Theology and Natural Science*. London: Archon Books, 1965.

Mikolaski, Samuel J. "The Triune God." Washington: *Christianity Today*, n.d.

Moorehead, Wm. G. "The Moral Glory of Jesus Christ a Proof of Inspiration," *The Fundamentals For Today*, Charles Feinberg, editor. Grand Rapids: Kregel, 1958.

Morris, Henry M. *The Bible Has The Answer*. Nutley, N. J.: The Craig Press, 1971.

Norris, J. Frank. *The "Virgin Birth."* New York: The Book Stall, n.d.

Northrup, Bernard E. "The Use of Almah in Isaiah 7:14." Unpublished master's thesis, Dallas Theological Seminary, 1955.

Orr, James, ed. *The International Standard Bible Encyclopaedia*. Grand Rapids: Wm. B. Eerdmans Publishing Co., 1952.

Orr, James. *The Virgin Birth of Christ*. New York: Charles Scribner's Sons, 1907. Reprinted by College Press, Joplin, Mo., 1972-73.

Payne, J. Barton. *The Theology of the Older Testament*. Grand Rapids: Zondervan Publishing House, 1962.

Pfeiffer, Charles F. and Harrison, Everett F., editors *The Wycliffe Bible Commentary*. Chicago: Moody Press, 1963.

Pike, Diane Kennedy and R. Scott Kennedy. *The Wilderness Revolt.* New York: Doubleday, 1972.

Ramm, Bernard. *Protestant Christian Evidences.* Chicago: Moody Press, 1959.

Ramm, Bernard. *The Christian View of Science and Scripture.* London: The Paternoster Press, 1967.

Rice, John R. *Immanuel.* Wheaton: Sword of the Lord Publishers, 1950.

Rice, John R. *Is Jesus God?* Murfreesboro, Tenn.: Sword of the Lord, 1964.

Robertson, A. T. *A Harmony of the Gospels.* New York: Harper Brothers, 1950.

Robertson, A. T. *Word Pictures in the New Testament.* Nashville: Broadman Press, 1930. 6 vols.

Robinson, John A. T. *But That I Can't Believe!* The New American Library, 1967.

Robinson, John A. T. *Honest to God.* Philadelphia: The Westminster Press, 1963.

Robinson, William Childs. "The Virgin Birth—A Broader Base," *Christianity Today,* Vol. XVII, No. 5 (December 8, 1972), pp. 6–8.

Sanders, Oswald J. *Cults and Isms.* Grand Rapids: Zondervan, 1962.

Sandmel, Samuel. *We Jews and Jesus.* New York: Oxford University Press, 1965.

Schaff, Philip. *The Creeds of Christendom.* Vol. I. New York: Harper and Brothers, 1877.

Shedd, William G. T. *Dogmatic Theology.* Grand Rapids: Zondervan, n.d. 3 vols.

Schneider, Johannes. "Jesus Christ: His Life and Ministry." Washington: Christianity Today, n.d.

Schonfield, Hugh J. *The Passover Plot.* New York: Bantam Books, 1967.

Schweitzer, Albert. *The Quest of the Historical Jesus.* New York: The Macmillan Company, 1950.

Smith, Wilbur M. *Therefore, Stand.* Boston: W. A. Wilde Co., 1950.

Smith, Wilbur M. *Supernaturalness of Christ.* Boston: W. A. Wilde Company, 1944.

Spivey, Robert A. and Smith, D. Moody, Jr. *Anatomy of the New Testament.* New York: Macmillan, 1969.

Sproul, R. C. *The Symbol.* Nutley, N. J.: The Presbyterian and Reformed Publishing Co., 1973.

Stonehouse, Ned B. *Origins of the Synoptic Gospels,* Grand Rapids: Wm. B. Eerdmans Publishing Co., 1963.

The Abingdon Bible Commentary. New York: The Abingdon Press, 1929.

The Interpreter's Bible. 12 vols. New York: Abingdon Press, 1951.

The Jewish Encyclopedia. New York: Funk and Wagnalls. 1906 12 vols.

Thielicke, Helmut. *Between Heaven and Earth.* New York: Harper & Row, 1965.

Tschudy, Earl H. *The Virgin Birth of Our Lord*. New York: Loizeaux Brothers, n.d.

Unger, Merrill F. *Unger's Bible Dictionary*. Chicago: Moody Press, 1957.

Walvoord, John F. *Jesus Christ Our Lord*. Chicago: Moody Press, 1969.

Walvoord, John F. "The Incarnation of the Son of God," *Bibliotheca Sacra*, Vol. 117, No. 465 (January, 1960).

Whale, J. S. *Christian Doctrine* London: Cambridge University Press, 1961.

Wilson, Robert Dick. "The Meaning of Alma (A.V. 'Virgin') in Isaiah VII. 14," *Princeton Theological Review*, Vol. 24, No. 2 (April, 1926).

Wolf, Herbert M. "A Solution to the Immanuel Prophecy in Isaiah 7:14—8:22, *Journal of Biblical Literature*, Vol. 91, No. 4 (December, 1972), pp. 449–456.